THE EU AND ROMANIA

Accession and Beyond

EDITED BY DAVID PHINNEMORE

Printed in the European Union

Contents

Illustrations

Contributors

Othon Anastaskis is Director of South East European Studies at Oxford (SEESOX), St Anthony's College, Oxford.

Traian Băsescu is President of Romania.

Sergiu Celac is currently Alternate Director General at the International Centre for Black Sea Studies in Athens having previously been Minister of Foreign Affairs (1989–1990), Ambassador to the United Kingdom (1990–1996), Ambassador-at-Large (1996–2000) and President of the Romanian Institute of International Relations (2000–2003).

Lazăr Comănescu has been Romania's Ambassador to the EU and Head of the Mission of Romania to the European Union since June 2001. Previously he was State Secretary for European Integration (1995–1998) and Head of the Mission of Romania to NATO (1998–2001).

Daniel Daianu is professor of economics at the School of Administrative and Political Studies (SNSPA) in Bucharest and former Finance Minister of Romania (1998) and Chief Economist of the National Bank of Romania (1992–1997).

Erhan İçener is a PhD candidate in the School of Politics, International Studies and Philosophy, Queen's University Belfast.

Valentin Lazea is Chief Economist at the National Bank of Romania

Duncan Light is Senior lecturer in Human Geography at Liverpool Hope University and co-editor with David Phinnemore of *Post-Communist Romania: Coming to Terms with Transition* (Palgrave, 2001)

Alina Mingiu-Pippidi is Director of the think-tank Romanian Academic Society, and the Freedom House analyst for Romania.

Dragoş Negrescu is Economic Analyst for the Delegation of the European Commission in Romania.

Baroness Nicholson of Winterbourne MEP has been Vice Chairman of the European Parliament's Committee on Foreign Affairs since her election in 1999. From 1999 to 2004 she was the rapporteur for Romania. Since 2004 she has been the shadow rapporteur for the Liberal Group in Parliament.

Leonard Orban is State Secretary in the Romanian Ministry of European Integration and was Deputy Chief Negotiator (2001–2004) for and later Chief Negotiator (2004–2005) for Romania's accession negotiations with the European Union.

David Phinnemore is Senior Lecturer in European Integration and Jean Monnet Chair of European Political Integration at the School of Politics, International Studies and Philosophy, Queen's University Belfast.

Adrian Severin is a Romanian Observer MEP at the European Parliament, was a representative of the Romanian Parliament at the European Convention and is a former Romanian Foreign Minister (1996–1997).

Alan Smith is Professor of Political Economy at the School of Slavonic and East European Studies, University College London.

Mihai-Răzvan Ungureanu has been Romania's Minister of Foreign Affairs since December 2004 and was previously deputy coordinator for the Southeast European Cooperation Initiative in Vienna (2003), Director General and Regional envoy of the Stability Pact for South-Eastern Europe (2001–2003) and State Secretary with the Ministry of Foreign Affairs (1998–2001).

Preface

TRAIAN BĂSESCU
PRESIDENT OF ROMANIA

I warmly welcome this volume on The EU and Romania which brings together the insights and views of a range of experts from across Europe. With Romania due to join the EU in 2007, its publication is timely and in the context of the renewed debate on enlargement, the subject of the book is highly topical.

Reading the volume was a pleasure for me, although I could not bring myself to agree fully with the views and opinions of all the authors. Despite this, I have learned something from each of the contributions. I was also left with the distinct feeling that the volume was shedding light on the complex relationship between a generic 'Europe' and one of its integral parts: Romania. The book is clearly inviting further reflection on and study of Romania as a member state of the EU. We should remember that Romania will be the seventh largest state in the enlarged EU(27), and a country which brings to the EU important assets, challenges as well as valuable lessons-learnt in the area of reform and transformation.

Those familiar with Romanian history, both old and recent, with its geography and development, with the country's progress and aspirations, are bound to admit that Romania is not the easiest subject to deal with. In my view, the challenges in understanding Romania stem from the many distinctive features which make it, in many respects, a case apart among Central and Eastern European countries.

The only Latin people in our part of the world, located on one of Huntington's 'fault lines', the border between Catholic and Orthodox Christianity, as well as Christianity and Islam, on the frontier between the Slavic and non-Slavic worlds, we Romanians have always regarded ourselves as Europeans, geographically, culturally, linguistically, and spiritually part of Europe. Beyond our undoubted Europeanness, our location as a gateway to the Black Sea, the frontier between the former Soviet area and the Balkans, have exposed us to multiple influences and granted us a rich, eventful and not always easy to grasp history. Our own Europeanness, unquestionable as it has been along the centuries, has always carried with it the reflection of the many links which Romania has had with European and non-European parts of the world.

More than 15 years after regaining freedom from communism and dictatorship, Romania is a NATO member and will shortly become a member of the EU. This book offers answers to many of the questions surrounding Romania's EU accession and membership.

To conclude, I would say that, among other things, the book uncovers a huge field for research waiting to be carried out. Therefore the initiative of the Federal Trust for Education and Research to publish the book is highly commendable. So is the Federal Trust's choice of the editor. David Phinnemore has been an outstanding expert in EU affairs, and Romania in particular, and his papers and books have offered to the politician, practitioner and student, valuable insight and information.

I wholeheartedly thank David Phinnemore, the editor of the volume, Brendan Donnelly, the Director of the Federal Trust for Education and Research, the publishing house I.B. Tauris, the contributors and everybody who has made possible the bringing together of such a stimulating and timely collection of assessments, reflections and predictions on Romania's relations with and forthcoming membership of the EU.

Acknowledgements

Compiling an edited volume on any aspect of the European Union today is a challenge and one that an editor can rarely do without inspiration and assistance. Thanks are therefore due to Brendan Donnelly of the Federal Trust for approaching me with the idea editing a volume on the EU and Romania and for then entrusting me with delivering on the project. Its completion would not have been possible without the support of staff at the Federal Trust. I wish in particular to thank Alexis Krachai for assisting in drawing together lists of possible contributors and for assisting with the administration of the project. Thanks are also due to Jonathan Church at the Federal Trust for his assistance in the production of the book and to the Embassy of Romania in London for recommending possible contributors and securing a number of contributions.

Abbreviations

ANP	Annual National Plan
BBC	British Broadcasting Company
BiH	Bosnia and Herzegovina
BSE	Bucharest Stock Exchange
BSEC	Black Sea Economic Cooperation
CAP	Common Agricultural Policy
CARDS	Community Assistance for Reconstruction, Development and Stabilisation
CDR	Romanian Democratic Convention
CEE	Central and Eastern European
CPI	consumer price index
DA	Justice and Truth
DG	Directorate-General
EC	European Community
ECJ	European Court of Justice
EEA	European Economic Area
EEC	European Economic Community
ENP	European Neighbourhood Policy
EP	European Parliament
ESDP	European Security and Defence Policy
EU	European Union
FDI	foreign direct investment
FDSN	Democratic Front of National Salvation
FSN	National Salvation Front
FYR	Former Yugoslav Republic (of Macedonia)
GATT	General Agreement of Tariffs and Trade
GDP	gross domestic product
ICA	inter country adoption
ICTY	International Criminal Tribunal for the former Yugoslavia
IMF	International Monetary Fund
IPA	Instrument of Pre-accession Assistance
JHA	justice and home affairs

MAP	Membership Action Plan
MEBO	management-employee buy-out
MEP	Member of the European Parliament
NAPCR	National Authority for the Protection of Child Rights
NATO	North Atlantic Treaty Organization
NBR	National Bank of Romania
NGO	non-governmental organization
OSCE	Organization for Security and Cooperation in Europe
PCR	Romanian Communist Party
PD	Democratic Party
PDSR	Party of Social Democracy of Romania
PfP	Partnership for Peace
PRM	Greater Romania Party
PSD	Social Democratic Party
PSM	Socialist Workers Party
R&D	research and development
RRA	Radio România Actualități
SAA	Stabilisation and Association Agreement
SAP	Stabilisation and Association Process
SECI	Southeast European Cooperation Initiative
SEE	South East European
SEECP	South-East European Cooperation Process
TVR	Romanian Television
UDMR	Democratic Union of the Hungarians of Romania
UK	United Kingdom
UN	United Nations
UNCRC	United Nations Convention on the Rights of the Child
UNICEF	Nations International Children's Emergency Fund
VAT	value added tax
WTO	World Trade Organization

Introduction

DAVID PHINNEMORE

Since the 'big bang' expansion of the European Union (EU) in 2004, political discussion and media coverage of enlargement have been dominated by the question of Turkey. Many people may therefore be excused if they are unaware that Bulgaria and Romania are scheduled to join the EU on 1 January 2007. Neither country's accession has received much attention beyond the occasional headline about corruption or migrant workers. Moreover, even if people are aware that the EU will soon be enlarging to 27 members, few are particularly conversant with the contexts, issues and challenges which have shaped the progress of Bulgaria and Romania towards accession. Few are aware either of what the two countries will bring to the EU. Filling some of the gaps that exist in people's awareness and understanding of one of the new member states – Romania – is the key purpose to this volume.

For many people, Romania, like most of the other countries that have acceded to the EU in recent years, is a country about which little is known and which they may not find easy to locate on a map of Europe. The violent events of December 1989 – Europe's only 'bloody' revolution – may have been televised around the world, but external media coverage of developments in the country since has been extremely limited. Some issues – corruption, child adoption, the situation of the Roma, for example – have attracted some attention. But reports on these cannot begin to convey either a balanced or rounded picture of the country as a whole or of the wide-ranging economic, political and social changes that have taken place since the collapse of the Ceaușescu regime. The extent of these changes should not be underestimated. In part driven by the desire for membership of the EU, the country has been transformed during the last decade. Democracy has established firm roots in the country. Economic stagnation and decline have been replaced by sustained growth. And standards of living have begun to rise. Nevertheless, except for those with a professional interest in Romania, few people would be particularly aware of such developments. For many people in Western Europe in particular, Romania is a relatively unknown country situated somewhere to the east.

Romania will, however, shortly become a member of the EU. On acceding to the EU Romania will nominate one it its nationals as a Commissioner, its citizens will gain representation in the European Parliament through 35

Romanian MEPs and, most importantly, the country will gain a voice and votes in the Council of Ministers and European Council. Romanians and Romania will therefore have opportunities to contribute to debates over the policies, priorities and future direction of the EU. They will bring their own ideas and perspectives to discussions, push their priorities, and seek to influence the EU's agenda.

In order to provide some insights into what sort of EU member state Romania might be and to discuss some of the consequences of its accession, this volume brings together a range of contributions from a distinguished collection of academics, parliamentarians and officials. Each has been asked to reflect, from their own perspective, on a key aspect of either Romania's journey to EU membership or its future position as a member. The contributions are organized in four broad sections. The first establishes the context of Romania's accession by providing an overview of historical, political and economic developments in the country as well as an overview of Romania's involvement in Euro-Atlantic processes since 1989. The second – The Road to the European Union – focuses on how Romania has fared in obtaining membership, whether in terms of economic or political reform or progress in accession negotiations. The third heading – Romania in the European Union – then brings together a range of perspectives on what Romania will bring to the EU and how membership will affect Romania. The final section – on Romania, the EU's New Neighbours and Enlargement – then explores some of the implications of Romania's accession for relations with the wider South-Eastern Europe region.

The context section opens with an overview of Romanian history during the last century and a half. Duncan Light traces the emergence of Romania as a modern state from the middle of the Nineteenth Century through the period of 'Greater Romania' in the inter-war years and on to the period of communist rule that eventually ended with the overthrow of the Ceauşescu regime in December 1989. Alina Mingiu-Pippidi then explores some of the key political developments in Romania since 1989, discussing the idea of Romanian 'exceptionalism' and the reasons why the country is now on the verge or EU membership. Particular attention is paid to the contribution of the early post-communist leader and three times president of Romania, Ion Iliescu, and to the EU as a force for political and economic change whose influence prevented Romania becoming a second 'Albania or Belarus'.

Romania's economic development since 1989 is then charted by Alan Smith who provides an overview of economic performance and the reform efforts of successive governments. His analysis highlights a range of factors, including the inheritance of post-communist Romania, to explain the relatively slow progress the county has made in establishing itself as a functioning market economy, an issue explored in more detail in Chapter 5 by Daniel Daianu. Attention is drawn by Smith to the role that external factors have played in accelerating the economic reform process, particularly since 2000. The chapter also focuses on the costs of transition where poverty levels and unemployment are concerned.

David Phinnemore concludes the context section by outlining developments in Romania's relations over the last decade and a half with the key organizations of the Euro-Atlantic integration process: the EU and NATO. The discussion shows how Romania gradually moved closer to membership of both organizations. This can be explained in part by Romania's own efforts to meet the relevant accession criteria and is in part due to the dynamics of the broader EU and NATO enlargement processes.

Specific issues affecting the progress of Romania towards EU membership are explored in more detail in the second section. Daniel Daianu's focus is the readiness of the Romanian economy for EU membership. He notes, on the one hand, the economic performance of the economy in recent years, the fact that 70% of Romanian trade is with the EU, and the expansion of the private sector in Romania, factors that would normally bode well. On the other hand, Daianu draws attention to the persistence of serious weaknesses in the Romanian economy (e.g. the need for pension reform, labour market rigidities) and warns of the dangers that exist if these are not addressed. Functioning domestic institutions will be crucial. The EU too has a role in acting as a force for modernization.

The role of the EU in encouraging reform is also dealt with by Baroness Nicholson of Winterbourne in her discussion on the state of the media and civil society in contemporary Romania. Drawing in particular on the issue of child protection, the chapter highlights the limited progress that has been made in Romania in developing civil society. The media may have become freer and journalistic standards improved, but its relative good health contrasts with that of Romanian civil society more generally. An over dependency on international funding by non-governmental organizations, exacerbated by a number of historical factors, has arguably restricted the emergence of the robust civil society that would be so beneficial to Romania society and politics.

The third contribution in this section is from Leonard Orban who provides an insider's perspective on the accession negotiations with the EU. Acknowledging Romania's laggard status compared to the rest of the Central and Eastern European countries, he outlines the nature of the negotiations and highlights the tremendous impact they had on the process of domestic reform in Romania in 2000–2004. Having discussed key phases in the negotiations, Orban outlines those chapters which proved the most difficult to negotiate:

free movement of capital, competition policy, the environment, and justice and home affairs. He concludes with a frank assessment of the main challenges that the Romania team faced in negotiating with the EU.

Having discussed aspects of Romania's progress towards accession, the volume's third section turns to what sort of EU member Romania will be. The first contribution is from Lazăr Comănescu who, having explored some of the reasons why Romania originally sought to join the EU, sets out Romania's interests and aspirations as it contemplates membership. In doing so, Comănescu highlights not only the potential economic gains from membership but also the challenges that integration has and will continue to pose for less competitive enterprises. Running through the chapter is the role that European integration and the quest for EU membership have had in encouraging and anchoring reform within Romania, processes that are set to continue after accession as integration further contributes to the post-1989 transformation of Romania.

Adrian Severin's chapter then offers a perspective on what Romania will bring to the EU – a question touched on too by Comănescu – and whether, owing to its size, it will be a big player among the smaller member states or a small player among the larger members. In support of his analysis he draws on the contributions that Romanian participants – himself included – made to the European Convention in 2002–2003, highlighting the constructive role that Romania can be expected to play as the EU addresses the question of the future of Europe.

The next two chapters focus on economic issues. Dragoș Negrescu examines the challenges that full participation in the Internal Market brings for Romania. Noting how much Romania is already integrated economically with the EU, Negrescu debunks the myth of a general 'integration shock' on accession. Adjustments have already been made in most areas although it is acknowledged that certain regimes (e.g. public procurement, capital movement, competition, taxation) still face challenges and will need to be adapted further. The adaptations are expected to have a positive impact. Valentin Lazea in his contribution on financial services is also conscious of the challenges that membership raises, particularly with regard to banking intermediation, competition within the banking sector, and the underdeveloped nature of the financial sector as a whole. Key to ensuring successful reform will be prudent macroeconomic policies.

The final contribution in this third section discusses what Romania's contribution will be to the EU's Common Foreign and Security Policy. Here Mihai-Răzvan Ungureanu outlines what Romania has already been contributing by way of political and military support to date. He then draws particular attention to Moldova and the Romanian wish to see increased EU engagement in resolving the Transnistria issue and more developed EU-Moldovan relations. More broadly, the European Neighbourhood Policy is welcomed and there is a call for a greater EU presence – through the European Security and Defence Policy – in the Black Sea region as well as EU support in resolving outstanding issues with Ukraine.

Ungureanu's contribution goes some way in setting the scene for the volume's final section on the significance of Romania's accession for the EU's relations – and those of Romania – with the EU's new neighbours and for the future of the enlargement process. Sergiu Celac begins with an assessment of priorities in the Black Sea area and with Russia. The former is seen as of vital strategic importance for the EU and Romania, given energy supplies emanating from the Caspian Sea. Celac therefore calls for a more constructive EU engagement with the Black Sea region and the development of existing cooperation instruments such as Black Sea Economic Cooperation. On Russia, he sees relations with Romania enhanced by a 2004 bilateral treaty. Like Ungureanu, he supports greater EU engagement with Moldova.

Erhan İçener then switches attention to Turkey. Having provided an overview of the country's relations with Romania, noting the positive level of economic and political cooperation, he offers an analysis of how Turkey's EU membership prospects might be affected by Romania's accession. Given the evident interest of Romania in an increased EU presence in the Black Sea area, it is clear that Turkey could benefit from Romania being inside the EU. But equally it is clear that Romania is giving greater priority to Moldova and the Western Balkans.

This brings us to the final contribution to the volume: that of Othon Anastaskis who reflects on the position of the Western Balkans in the EU's enlargement process and on some of the lessons countries in this region might learn from Romania's experiences of moving towards membership of the EU. The chapter reminds us not only that enlargement does not end with the accession Bulgaria and Romania, but more importantly that it is a dynamic process.

These contributions go some way to providing a sense of how Romania will have soon achieved membership of the EU and what sort of member state it will be. It is evident that the road to membership has been a difficult and challenging one for Romania. A range of legacies and obstacles have had to be overcome. Some still remain. And, as several of the chapters reveal, various challenges and difficulties will persist well after Romania has acceded to the EU. Moreover, membership itself will not bring an end to EU demands for reform and change. As the governments and the citizens of those states that joined in 2004 would no doubt testify, dealing with the realities of EU membership can be as challenging as meeting the criteria of accession, if not more so. Membership obviously has its advantages though. On acceding to the EU, Romania will have its voice heard, will gain influence, and will become a fuller participant in the European integration process. It will have greater opportunities to shape the activities and to contribute to the development of the EU. Ideas clearly exist of what Romania may and will seek as an EU member. How successful Romania will be in seizing opportunities to promote and develop its preferences and priorities remains to be seen.

Context

CHAPTER ONE

Modern Romania: An Historical Overview

Duncan Light

ROMANIA AFTER INDEPENDENCE

Romania first appeared on the map of Europe as an independent state in 1878. During the previous two decades Romania – then comprising the regions of Wallachia and Moldova – had enjoyed a form of semi-independence within the ailing Ottoman Empire, its status guaranteed by the major European powers. Indeed, the Romanians had made considerable progress towards full statehood. The first elected parliament met in Bucharest in 1862 and in 1866 the country had acquired a figurehead (and considerable prestige) when Prince Karl (Carol in Romanian) of Hohenzollern had accepted the invitation to assume the newly established Romanian throne. During the 1877 Russo-Turkish war in which Romania allied itself with Russia, the Romanian parliament declared its independence from the Ottoman Empire. The following year this status was confirmed by the Congress of Berlin.

The newly created Romania was far from being a true nation-state. On the one hand there were sizable non-Romanian minorities among the population of nearly 4 million people. The largest was the Jewish minority that comprised around 3% of the population overall, and considerably more in Moldova. On the other hand there was a large Romanian population outside Romania. Most (over 2 million) of them lived in Transylvania, then part of the Austro-Hungarian Empire, where they considerably outnumbered Magyars (Hungarians). But there were also large Romanian populations in Bucovina (also under Austro-Hungarian control) and Bessarabia (under Russian control after 1878). The establishment of Romania as an independent state inevitably gave a further stimulus to nationalist movements in these regions that sought unification with Romania.

Romania in 1878 was something of a paradox. The ruling elite were enthusiastically modern in outlook and looked westwards. During the middle and late nineteenth century Romania drew on European models for its constitution, parliamentary system, public administration, judicial system, education, universities, literary, artistic and architectural forms and even styles of clothing. France – a Latin 'sister' – was the strongest role model. Even the Romanian language was 'Westernised': the Cyrillic alphabet was replaced by the Latin one in 1860, while numerous words of Slavic origin were dropped and replaced by their French equivalents.

Notwithstanding its enthusiasm for all things Western, Romania in 1878 had little in common with the states of Western Europe. The level of economic development was low and almost pre-capitalist in nature. Industry accounted for just 3% of employment (compared with over 30% in Germany). The degree of urbanisation was similarly low: only around 15% of the population lived in towns (compared with over 30% in France and around 70% in Britain). Most Romanians lived in rural areas and worked in agriculture. However, conditions in the countryside were almost feudal in nature due to the dominance of large, absentee landowners.

Moreover, despite the trappings of parliamentary democracy, Romania was far from being a democratic state. Only 2% of the population had the right to a direct vote and the rural population was effectively disenfranchised. Romania became a Kingdom in 1881 and under the rule of King Carol a rather unique system of governance emerged, whereby two parties – Conservative and Liberal – would alternate in power, their tenure lasting until the King decided it was time for a change. Romania's ruling oligarchy was primarily concerned to protect the interests of particular client groups (the Conservatives represented large landowners while the Liberals represented smaller property owners, the civil service and the emerging middle class) but showed little interest in the welfare of the majority rural population.

Romania under Carol experienced an unprecedented period of stability. This was a period of consolidation for the new state. New institutions were created, including the Romanian Academy (1879), the National Bank (1880) and the Stock Exchange (1881). The armed forces were strengthened, education was reorganised and infrastructure and communications improved. Legislation was introduced to stimulate industrial development and foreign investment. Industrial production – particularly the extraction and processing of raw materials (including petrol) – increased and Romania experienced steady, if unspectacular economic development.

The period after 1878 was one of confidence and creativity in cultural life. New newspapers and journals were established and many writers, poets, dramatists, literary critics, artists and musicians rose to prominence. At the forefront of this cultural revival was the 'Junimea' society, founded in Iaşi in 1863, which nurtured and encouraged some of Romania's finest writers, among them the 'national poet' Mihai Eminescu and the dramatist Ion Luca Caragiale. Members of Junimea were sceptical about the ruling elite's enthusiasm for all things Western and the literary critic Titu Maiorescu famously coined the expression 'form without substance' to describe the formal but superficial imitation of Western models.

The stability that Romania enjoyed after independence appeared set to continue into the Twentieth Century. However, the problems of the rural areas, particularly land shortages among a growing and impoverished rural population, remained unresolved and exploded in 1907 in a peasants' uprising. This was brutally repressed and many thousands of peasants were killed. Nevertheless, the events jolted the political elite out of its denial that there was a rural problem and some attempt was made at agrarian reform after 1907. Romanian peasants fought for the Romanian army in the Second Balkan War in 1913 (in which Bulgaria went to war with its neighbours) and came to recognise the better conditions enjoyed by their counterparts in Bulgaria, further increasing the pressure for both constitutional and agrarian reforms. The Balkan War itself brought Romania its first territorial change since 1878 when it gained Southern Dobrogea from Bulgaria (see Figure 1.1), even though most of the population of this region was not Romanian.

The First World War and its Aftermath

Romania initially declared its neutrality at the start of the First World War. Given the Francophilia of many Romanians, an alliance with France seemed the obvious course of action. However, because of his German background, King Carol was inevitably reluctant to go to war against Germany. The situation changed with Carol's death in October 1914 and his successor, Ferdinand, was more inclined towards supporting the Triple Entente of France, Britain and Russia. Romania's position was underpinned by the prospect of territorial gains at the end of the war, and many politicians had an eye on Transylvania. In 1916 the Entente powers concluded an agreement that promised Romania the territories of Transylvania, Banat and Bucovina in return for declaring war on Austria-Hungary.

Romania entered the war in August 1916. After initial progress, Romanian forces were put on the defensive and Romania was effectively conquered (German forces occupied Bucharest in late 1916). Romania was out of the war until events took an unexpected turn in the summer of 1918 when the collapse

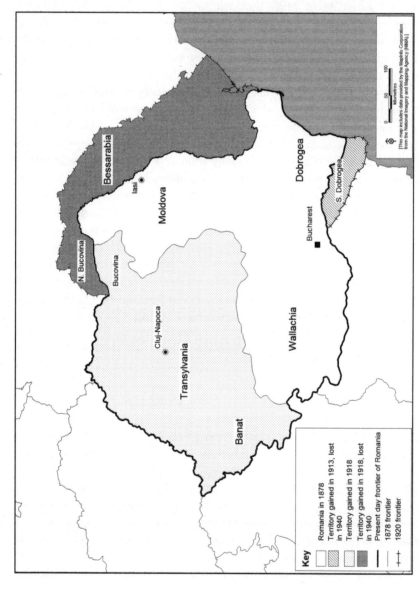

Key

	Romania in 1878
	Territory gained in 1913, lost in 1940
	Territory gained in 1918
	Territory gained in 1918, lost in 1940
—	Present day frontier of Romania
—	1878 frontier
+‒+	1920 frontier

1.1 Modern Romania

of Germany and Austria-Hungary appeared imminent. At this point, Romania renewed hostilities and in November, Romanian armies entered Bucovina and Transylvania. As the Austro-Hungarian Empire collapsed, Romanians in Bucovina declared union with Romania on 28 November. Three days later the union of Transylvania with Romania was proclaimed in the Transylvanian town of Alba Iulia. Since 1990, 1 December has been Romania's national day in commemoration of what Romanians know as the 'Great Union'.

After protracted bargaining at the Paris peace conference of 1919 Romania's territorial gains were largely confirmed, due in part to the interventions of Ferdinand's wife, the British-born Queen Marie. After the War Romania had gained Transylvania, Bessarabia (which had voted for union with Romania in April 1918), Bucovina and the eastern part of the Banat (see Figure 1.1) – far more than even the most optimistic could have foreseen at the start of the war. The new state became known as Greater Romania (*România Mare*). Romania had more than doubled in area (making it now the tenth largest state in Europe) and its population had increased from 7.5 million to 16 million.

THE INTER-WAR PERIOD

After the War, Romania's ruling elite was faced with the task of organising and consolidating the much expanded state. Since the peasantry had valiantly fought in the Romanian army during the war and increasingly regarded themselves as citizens of Greater Romania, their demands could no longer be ignored. Legislation introduced by the Liberals in 1921 brought about long overdue reforms, notably universal male suffrage and agrarian restructuring in which the large estates were broken up and the land redistributed among the peasantry. One of the casualties of rural reform was the Conservative Party which disappeared from the political scene in 1922. With it also went the two-party system that had been the bedrock of political life since independence.

Instead, Romania came to resemble a multi-party democracy, albeit with a highly fragmented political landscape. A plethora of new parties appeared, reflecting the diversity of views among the much expanded electorate (the 1937 elections were contested by 13 major parties and 54 secondary organisations). Nevertheless, Romanian politics in the interwar period were dominated by the Liberal Party, with the Transylvania based National Peasant Party representing the main opposition. Once again, Romania was an imperfect democracy, since electoral fraud was an accepted practice. The one exception was the election of 1928, which was probably the first time since 1866 that Romania had experienced a truly free election.

Greater Romania was much more ethnically diverse than the pre-War Kingdom: 72% of the population was Romanian but there were also significant Hungarian, German, Jewish, Ukrainian, Russian and Bulgarian minorities. However, Greater Romania was built on the doctrine of the 'unitary state' and consequently there were few concessions to regional identities or to non-Romanian minorities. Instead, the emphasis was on unifying the territory and people of the new state. Hence, various measures were introduced that were intended to assimilate the minority groups, including a highly centralised administration that permitted no local autonomy. Hungarians in Transylvania were dismissed *en masse* from public sector employment and their jobs given to Romanians. Similarly, the centuries-old system of local administration that the German (Saxon) community in Transylvania had enjoyed was dismantled.

The expansion of Romania considerably increased the country's economic potential. The much-enlarged agricultural area enabled Romania once again to become a major producer and exporter of grain (even though agricultural reform had created a plethora of small and inefficient farms) and by the 1930s Romania was the fifth largest agricultural producer in the world. However, there was increasing economic diversification and a move away from an economy dominated by agriculture. The state introduced new policies to encourage and support the development of industry and during the 1920s and 1930s Romania had one of the highest industrial growth rates in the world. Food processing was the largest industry, with other notable sectors including oil production and refining (oil products were Romania's main export), metallurgy, chemicals, engineering, textiles and forestry. Nevertheless, to put things into perspective, by 1930 only around 10% of the population was employed in industry (with over 70% continuing to work in agriculture) and only around 20% of Romanians lived in towns. Greater Romania, like the pre-War Kingdom, was a modern European state in appearance but less so in reality.

The inter-war period also witnessed a great flowering of artistic, cultural and scientific activity, testifying to the confidence of Romania at this time. Among the best-known names are the sculptor Constantin Brâncuși and the musician George Enescu. There was similar creativity in the sciences: the Romanian school of mathematics acquired international prestige; Romanian aviators contributed significantly to the development of powered flight; and Romanian doctors also made important contributions to the development of medicine.

However, for all the achievements of Greater Romania, the state was increasingly destabilised by internal developments. A key role was played by the rise of the extreme Right. During the 1920s a Moldavian law graduate, Corneliu Zelea Codreanu, had founded the 'Legion of the Archangel Michael', a movement dedicated to the regeneration of Romania. The Legion's platform was nationalist, anti-Semitic and anti-European in nature. It stressed the superiority of native Romanian values (especially those derived from Romanian Orthodox Church traditions) and an almost mystical idealisation of the Romanian peasantry. The Legion appealed to a broad spectrum of Romanian society. Some were disillusioned with corrupt and ineffective parliamentary politics and were attracted by the disciplined and authoritarian approach of the Legion; others were in sympathy with the Legion's anti-Semitic and anti-Communist stance; others regarded it as the only political movement concerned to improve the situation of the peasantry. The Legion also appealed to many of the leading intellectuals of the day, who were drawn to its stress on indigenous rather than European values. In 1930 the Legion established a political wing that became known as the Iron Guard.

At the same time, Romania's imperfect parliamentary system came under attack from King Carol II. The son of Ferdinand and Marie, Carol's conduct was such that he had been forced to renounce his claim to the throne in 1923 (he had deserted the front during World War One, and later abandoned his wife to take a divorcee as his mistress). After Ferdinand's death in 1927, a Regency Council ruled on behalf of Carol's six-year-old son, Mihai. In 1930, Carol returned from exile and persuaded the government of the day to reinstate him as King. He immediately demonstrated his inclination for a personal and authoritarian style of rule and set about undermining parliamentary democracy. He adopted a practice of appointing prime ministers and sacking them almost immediately. Between 1930 and 1940 Romania had 18 different heads of government. Carol instead surrounded himself with acolytes and increasingly plundered the country's wealth for his personal gain.

Given his authoritarian tendencies Carol's sympathies were with the Right and he tacitly supported the Iron Guard. Consequently the Legion was able to become an increasingly active political force, frequently resorting to violence to achieve its ends. Legionaries assassinated the prime minister in 1933. The movement became ever more hostile towards the King who recognised that he could exert little control over it. Consequently, on 10 February 1938 Carol declared a Royal Dictatorship, an event that is widely regarded as marking the inglorious end of Greater Romania. All political parties apart from Carol's 'National Renaissance Front' were dissolved and Carol attempted to stamp out the Legion, resulting in the imprisonment and assassination of Codreanu. The Legionaries responded by assassinating the prime minister in 1939 and continued to destabilise Carol's regime.

THE SECOND WORLD WAR

King Carol did his best to stay out of the looming European conflict and to maintain good relations with France, Britain and Germany. As such, Romania declared itself neutral when the Second World War broke out. However, with the fall of France, Romania faced the unenviable choice of siding with either Hitler's Germany or Stalin's Soviet Union. In any case events were beyond Carol's control, particularly since Romania's neighbours were now in a position to reclaim territories they had unwillingly surrendered after the First World War. In June 1940 Stalin (with Hitler's agreement) demanded the annexation of Bessarabia and Northern Bucovina. Carol had little choice but to accede. In August the Vienna Diktat forced Romania to cede northern Transylvania to another of Hitler's allies, Hungary (which had never accepted the loss of Transylvania and had long sought its recovery). In September, Bulgaria reclaimed Southern Dobrogea. Most of Greater Romania had now been dismantled (see Figure 1.1). For Carol, these territorial losses were a blow from which he never recovered. Facing mounting hostility, the King granted dictatorial powers to an army officer, General Ion Antonescu, before abdicating and fleeing the country, leaving the throne to his son Mihai.

Although Antonescu was not naturally sympathetic to Germany his main concern was to restore internal order after the chaos of Carol's dictatorship and to preserve Romania's territorial integrity as far as possible. Romania therefore allied itself with Germany and, in an attempt to satisfy the demands of the Legionaries, Antonescu brought the Iron Guard (which now enjoyed Nazi support) into government to form what was known as the 'national Legionary state'. The Legionaries proved unreliable partners, and frequently resorted to violence, much of it directed at Romania's Jewish community. Thus, in early 1941 Antonescu moved decisively against the Iron Guard: many of its members were imprisoned (some were executed) and the movement itself was outlawed. The short-lived national Legionary state came to an end and Antonescu ruled alone by military dictatorship.

Thereafter, Romania fought with the Germans on the Eastern front. Romanian armies recaptured Bessarabia and Northern Bucovina, but pushed on further eastwards into Soviet territory, reaching Odessa in the Crimea and fighting alongside the Germans at Stalingrad. In these territories Nazi policies towards the Jews were implemented: many Jews were killed in summary executions, while over 150,000 were deported to camps where most died. Antonescu's approach towards the Jews was ambivalent. Although he was certainly anti-Semitic he ignored German orders to deport the Jewish population from southern Romania, where almost all Jews survived (in the Hungarian controlled parts of Transylvania Jews were deported to death camps in Poland). At the end of the war the Jewish population was around 350,000, out of a population of 650,000 before the war.

Following the German defeat at Stalingrad, Romania's fortunes changed dramatically. The Red Army pushed westwards and by 1944 had retaken Bessarabia and Bucovina. By this stage Antonescu was looking for ways to leave the war but was unable to agree terms with the Allies. In May 1944 the Soviet Union invaded Romania. Facing total occupation by the Red Army, King Mihai organised a *coup d'état* against Antonescu on 23 August 1944. Romania changed sides and declared war against Germany, an action that probably shortened the war by six months. Within a week Soviet forces had arrived in Bucharest and taken control of the country. The Romanian army now entered northern Transylvania, which was liberated by late October. Treaties at the end of the war confirmed Transylvania as Romanian territory, but Southern Dobrogea was retained by Bulgaria, northern Bucovina was incorporated into Soviet Ukraine, and Bessarabia became the Soviet Republic of Moldova.

COMMUNIST ROMANIA

At the Yalta conference of February 1945 Stalin and Churchill reached their famous 'percentages agreement' in which Churchill agreed to give the Soviet Union a free hand in Romania in return for staying out of Greece. In any case Romania was now an occupied country and Stalin lost no time bringing it under Soviet control and installing the Romanian Communist Party (PCR) in power. The party had been founded in 1921 but had always occupied a marginal position in Romanian political life. All of a sudden, it found itself in a position to shape Romania's future. With Soviet backing communists increasingly took control of Romania using a combination of intimidation, manipulation of the democratic process and outright violence. The first communist-dominated government was formed in March 1945 while in blatantly forged elections of November 1946 the communists and their allies took 80% of the vote. By late 1947 the last obstacle to a complete takeover of power was King Mihai. On 30 December the King was forced at gunpoint to abdicate and the People's Republic of Romania was proclaimed.

Under the leadership of Gheorghe Gheorghiu-Dej, a man as ruthless as he was cynical, the communists set about a complete political, economic, social and cultural transformation of Romania. Dej pursued a policy of undeviating loyalty to Stalin making Romania the most pliant of the Soviet satellites in Eastern Europe. Single party rule was introduced and many of the leaders of the pre-war democratic parties were imprisoned. Industries, mines, transport, banks, cinemas and health institutions were nationalised in 1948–9 while private land ownership was abolished in 1949 and the process of agricultural collectivisation started. The market economy was replaced by central planning with the first Five Year Plan being introduced in 1951. Following Stalin, industrialisation was seen as the key to modernisation and successive plans provided for extensive investment in heavy industry.

The communists also set about creating a new society: this meant completely recasting Romanian national values and history. Education was reorganised to stress Marxist principles. Censorship was introduced and thousands of books considered unsuitable were withdrawn. Romanian history was entirely rewritten to stress the Slavic (particularly Russian) influence on Romania's development, while at the same time Western influences were downplayed or denied altogether. Even the Romanian language was revised to make it appear more Slavic and less Latin in origin. The rewriting of history also greatly exaggerated the role of the PCR in the country's history. Perhaps the best example was the reinterpretation of the 1944 *coup* that had over-thrown Antonescu: this was now presented as solely the achievement of the PCR and 23 August became Romania's national day during the communist period.

In addition, since the communist regime lacked legitimacy and popular support a powerful internal security service – the *Securitate* – was needed to maintain order. Many of those who opposed the regime or who were considered in any way to be suspect – including those associated with the Antonescu era, landowners, intellectuals, students, members of non-Romanian minorities, and peasants who had resisted collectivisation – were either sent into internal exile or put to work in forced labour camps. An estimated 180,000 people worked in such camps by the early 1950s, the most notorious of which was the Danube-Black Sea canal project. Within a short space of time the Romanian population was terrorised into acceptance of, and submission towards, the communist regime.

After Stalin's death, Romania maintained a policy of total loyalty to the Soviet Union. However, in the 1960s a Soviet planner proposed an economic division within the Soviet bloc, whereby some countries would specialise in industry and others in agriculture. Romania was allocated a predominantly agricultural role, something that was unacceptable to the country's leadership. The proposal was later abandoned, but it caused a major change in Romania's relations with Moscow. Dej started to distance Romania from the Soviet Union and to stress Romania's national interests instead. This resulted in a campaign of 'de-Russification' and the rewriting yet again of Romanian history to re-assert Romanian national values. In 1964 the leadership issued a 'declaration of independence' which asserted Romania's right to determine its own course of development.

In 1965 Dej died and was succeeded by a little known apparatchik, Nicolae Ceaușescu. One of Ceaușescu's first actions was to rename the country the 'Socialist Republic of Romania'. The new General Secretary appeared young and energetic and prepared to embrace change. He denounced the excesses of the Dej era and the early years of his rule seemed to promise a more open and liberal Romania. Censorship was relaxed, Western newspapers were available in Bucharest, Western films and television programmes were shown and even a Pepsi-Cola bottling plant opened in 1968. Ceaușescu continued Dej's policy of maintaining Romania's independence from the Soviet Union. This was most spectacularly demonstrated in August 1968 when the Soviet Union, supported by forces from other Warsaw Pact countries, invaded Czechoslovakia to crush the 'Prague spring'. Ceaușescu called a rally in Bucharest in which he denounced the invasion as an act of Russian aggression. This defiance brought Ceaușescu massive and apparently genuine popularity within Romania.

Ceaușescu's actions in 1968 brought him the attention and respect of the West. They were followed by invitations for official visits to Western countries (including the USA and the United Kingdom in 1978). Ceaușescu increasingly sought to present himself as a reforming communist, pursuing an independent foreign policy within the Soviet Bloc. He was also eager to be seen as an enlightened international statesman, able to mediate in international conflicts, a leader capable of gaining international respect for Romania. For much of the 1970s, the West bought into this myth. However, Ceaușescu's reputation became increasingly tarnished during the 1980s and when Mikhail Gorbachev appeared on the scene in the Soviet Union, Ceaușescu appeared as an unreformed Stalinist dinosaur.

Domestically Ceaușescu never lived up to the promise of the early years of his rule. Following a visit to China and North Korea in 1971 he implemented a new wave of censorship and repression, whilst also setting in motion the formation of a grotesque personality cult. Ceaușescu was increasingly lauded as the embodiment of wisdom and national genius; at the same time, historians and poets compared Ceaușescu with the medieval princes, presenting the dictator as the latest and greatest in a long line of heroes who had fought for Romania's independence. The hagiographers also turned Ceaușescu's wife, Elena, into an academic chemist of global fame, even though she had left school with no qualifications. Power was increasingly concentrated in the hands of Ceaușescu and his family, while second tier officials were constantly rotated in order to prevent the establishment of any alternative power base.

Stalin-like, Ceaușescu continued to prioritise the expansion of heavy industry. This entailed importing vast quantities of raw materials thus running up large foreign debts. However, because the quality of the country's industrial output was always poor Romania was unable to export to the West. At the same time, the production of consumer goods for the domestic market was neglected, frustrating the demands of the population for an improved standard of living. Ceauşescu refused any decentralisation of the planning system or any reforms that might have allowed a greater role for the market (as had been introduced in neighbouring Hungary). Indeed, Ceauşescu continually interfered in economic matters introducing a seemingly irrational dimension into the planning process.

Ceauşescu also resorted to an increasingly strident and xenophobic nationalism which was directed particularly at the non-Romanian minorities (especially Hungarians) within the state. Under the slogan 'Romanians must be masters in their own home' the regime set about assimilating its minorities. Romanians were therefore moved into towns and cities with a large Hungarian population; Hungarian language schools were closed or marginalised; and Hungarian graduates were assigned jobs in overwhelmingly Romanian areas. As a result, many Hungarians and Germans chose to emigrate rather than remain in Romania.

Ceauşescu's Romania got progressively bleaker during the 1980s. The economy was underperforming to the extent that Romania had to import food from the West. By 1981 Romania's foreign debt had risen to $10.2 billion. Driven by a misplaced nationalist pride and an aversion to dependence on the West, Ceauşescu decided to pay off the entire foreign debt ahead of schedule. The result was unprecedented austerity and hardship for ordinary Romanians. Almost all food was exported resulting in domestic food shortages, while imports were stopped. Heating and lighting in homes and workplaces were also rationed. To quell internal dissent the *Securitate* became ever more repressive: Romanians came to believe that all telephones were bugged and that up to one in three of the population was a police informer.

Despite the looming crisis Ceauşescu became increasingly detached from reality. The dictator embarked on a draconian scheme to remodel Bucharest. Around 5 km^2 of the historic city were razed and in their place a modern 'civic centre' and an enormous monumental building known as the 'House of the People' were built. Ceauşescu also announced a scheme to 'systematise' rural areas that would have resulted in the destruction of around 6000 villages and the displacing of their population to new 'agro-industrial' towns. The international community increasingly shunned the paranoid dictator who was increasingly known as the 'sick man of communism'.

THE 1989 REVOLUTION

As communist regimes collapsed throughout Central and Eastern Europe in the autumn of 1989, only Romania under Ceauşescu seemed prepared to resist. Indeed, events such as the fall of the Berlin Wall were not even reported in Romania. But in western Romania the population had access to Hungarian and Yugoslav television and had been able to follow wider events in the region. On 15 December 1989 a protest broke out in the western city of Timişoara against the removal of a dissident Hungarian priest. Romanians joined Hungarians in what quickly mounted into a full-scale insurrection. The regime's response was characteristically brutal: troops opened fire on demonstrators, killing and wounding hundreds.

Believing that he had contained the uprising Ceauşescu called for a public rally of support in Bucharest on 21 December. Speaking from the same balcony at which he had made his famous 1968 speech, the dictator was jeered and heckled by the crowd and the astonishment of the feeble old man was broadcast live on television. Crowds gathered in the streets and during the night the security forces opened fire killing 49 people and injuring over 450. The following day, protestors stormed the Central Committee building inside which Ceauşescu had taken refuge, forcing the dictator and his wife to flee from the roof by helicopter. Forces loyal to Ceauşescu opened fire on the crowds, while the army declared itself on the side of the people and joined the revolution. The dramatic street fighting that followed was caught by television crews from around the world making what happened in Romania the world's first televised revolution. A group describing itself as the National Salvation Front, led by a veteran communist, Ion Iliescu, took power, ostensibly in the name of the people. It committed itself to pluralist government, free elections, the establishment of a market economy and respect for the country's minorities. Meanwhile, the Ceauşescus had been captured: they were later tried and executed by a firing squad. The video of their death was shown repeatedly on Romanian television on Christmas Day to convince all in the country that Ceauşescu's regime really had come to an end. Over one thousand Romanians lost their lives in the course of the revolution and a further 3,300 were injured.

Soon after the Ceauşescu's overthrow rumours circulated that what had happened was not a mass popular revolution, but some sort of pre-planned *coup d'état* by a group of reform-minded communists, intent on overthrowing Ceauşescu but not abandoning communism. Romanians started talking about the 'stolen', 'unfinished' or 'so-called' Revolution. Many of the events of December 1989 are still clouded in confusion and what really happened may never be fully known. But the fact remains that the Romanian people mobilised to overthrow a particularly unpleasant dictator and bring about a major transfer of power. The events set Romania on the course to a new, but uncertain future.

SOURCES

Boia, L. *Romania: Borderland of Europe* (London: Reaktion Books, 2001)
Deletant, D. *Romania Under Communist Rule* (Iaşi: Center for Romanian Studies, 1999)
Georgescu, V. *The Romanians: A History* (London: I.B. Tauris, 1991)
Rady, M. *Romania in Turmoil* (London: I.B. Tauris, 1992)
Siani-Davies, P. *The Romanian Revolution of December 1989* (London: Cornell University Press, 2005)
Treptow, K. (ed) *A History of Romania* (Iaşi: Center for Romanian Studies, 1996)
Turnock, D. *An Economic Geography of Romania* (London: G Bell and Sons, 1974)

CHAPTER TWO

Europeanization without Decommunization: a case of elite conversion

Alina Mungiu-Pippidi

Since its spectacular 1989 'televised Revolution', Romania has spent most of its political transition struggling with its own past. For political scientists, these confusing times only confirmed what they had already labelled as Romanian 'exceptionalism',[1] a pattern dissimilar from Central European countries. However, in the early 1990s, Romania's ways were not so exceptional when compared to Belarus or Albania – it was just another case where the exit path from a totalitarian regime did not lead to democracy, but instead to some form of mild authoritarian populism. With the benefit of hindsight, what is exceptional and needs some explanation in Romania's case is not her difficult separation with its communist past, but the final positive outcome: the signing of the Accession Treaty with the European Union (EU) in April 2005. Despite important similarities with countries such as Belarus and Albania at the beginning of its transition, why has Romania done so well by comparison? In McFaul's classification, Romania is the only post-communist country which succeeded in becoming a consolidated democracy with a balance of power clearly in favour of the former communist elites.[2] This invites some explanation.

Any account of Romania's political transition has to answer two basic questions. The first is why did a country barely liberated from Ceauşescu endorse socialism and prefer former communists as leaders in the initial years of its transition when its Central European neighbours were rapidly advancing

[1] Linz, J.J. and Stepan, A. *Problems of Democratic Transition and Consolidation* (Baltimore: The John Hopkins University Press, 1996).

[2] McFaul, M. 'The Fourth Wave of Democracy and Dictatorship: Non-Cooperative Transitions in the Post-communist world', *World Politics*, 54 (2) 2002, 212–244.

with the deep and complex transformation of their societies? The second, and closely related question, is what brought about the disenchantment with this Romanian 'Third Way' and led to the emergence of pro-reform, pro-European, and more pragmatically oriented governments? This chapter will address these questions in turn.

CONJECTURAL EXPLANATIONS OR ORIGINAL SINS

Romania's politics after its 1989 'entangled revolution'[3] can be roughly divided into two phases. The first was a phase of democratization, following the only 'revolution' in Central and Eastern Europe which did not bring about a victory of anti-communists in elections. Ion Iliescu, a former communist leader, and his populist National Salvation Front (FSN), which campaigned with slogans against party politics and Western capitalism, won an overwhelming victory after free but unfair elections in May 1990. The second was the phase of consolidation, which started with the peaceful departure from power of Iliescu in 1996, after he lost elections to a coalition formed by anti-communists and deserters from his own party. He returned to the Presidency in 2000, but this did nothing to change what was then Romania's EU accession course.

By the Thirteenth Congress of the Romanian Communist Party (PCR) in November 1989, Romania had only a few, isolated dissidents. In fact, some were actually former communists. However, political mobilization had attained unprecedented levels: by 1989, Romania had 4 million party members, a third of the adult population, more than double the average percentage in the Soviet bloc. While in the Universities of Ljubljana or Warsaw many faculty members were not party members, not one student could register for a PhD program in Romania by the late 1980s without a PCR membership card. The entire faculty were party members. Clearly, the party membership card had become a sort of driving license, a convenience tool. The 1980s brought a tremendous deterioration in life standards, with the collapse of heating systems and shortages of basic goods, putting Romania in a specific situation: no organized opposition, a huge party, but widespread hatred of Ceauşescu's regime, even among its own party members. Listening to Radio Free Europe, which was forbidden, was the only, but generally widespread, act of opposition.

The uprising of December 1989 seemed anarchical. It would not have started at all had Ceauşescu not come up with the bad idea of gathering a demonstration in his support against the rebellion in Timişoara. There might have been, as hypothesized later, some agents to prompt protests who worked for some

[3]   See Ratesh, N. *Romania: The Entangled Revolution* (Boulder Co.: Praeger Publishers, 1991).

foreign intelligence agency, as well as some secret police = *Securitate* = officers who acted as revolutionaries and got themselves elected in the provisional 'national salvation' bodies. An *ad hoc* structure was created in the overrun central office of the PCR. This included a few dissidents, among which was Iliescu, a well-known opponent of Ceausescu from within the Party. This body announced that very same evening its first decree, granting the people every freedom = travel, association, protest and speech = as well as free elections.

Although clear proof is missing of a plot between Iliescu and Ceausescu's repressive structures, the following days had a marked resemblance with Lenin's teachings on how to organize a *coup d'état*. First, Iliescu was elected president of the *ad hoc* revolutionary body, the FSN, and started to sign decrees in his own name. Second, to avoid 'anarchy', he encouraged people to elect management bodies throughout the country to replace the old PCR ones. All of these hierarchical structures of the FSN he turned overnight into a political party and announced his intention to compete in forthcoming elections against the other parties, which were just beginning to form. Protesting in the streets became impossible in those crucial days due to sniper fire, which kept Bucharest's people indoors for over ten days. Ceausescu was arrested fast and executed after a summary trial on December 25, allegedly in order to discourage the snipers from continuing resistance. As no snipers have ever been tried, and no serious investigation has been performed to find out who shot during those days, killing hundreds in Bucharest only, the most anti-communist section of the population has become convinced that this diversion was organized by Iliescu himself to allow him to control the popular movement. The hard fact remains that Iliescu consolidated his position after 22 December with the support of former repressive agencies = the Army and the *Securitate* = which badly needed to find a moderate leader able to channel the popular anger directed against them. He also controlled the state TV, and won the popular vote in May 1990 despite continuous street protests. To control the Bucharest opposition that remained in the streets even after the elections, Iliescu resorted to vigilante groups, such as the coal miners, who in June 1990 beat protesters in University Square, destroyed part of the University of Bucharest and the offices of opposition parties and the free media, all with the tacit endorsement of the police.

The FSN was initially a mix of spontaneous elements and *Securitate* agents. After the May 1990 elections, however, three former nomenklatura members managed to secure the Presidency and the presidencies of the Senate and the Chamber of Deputies. The FSN did not start as the typical communist successor party, claiming instead a revolutionary birth. Yet its nature was fully revealed after the May 1990 elections, as the *ad hoc*, revolutionary elements lost all important positions – they later split and formed the Democratic Party

(PD) = and many conservative communist elements were rehabilitated. This process was completed fully after a new round of elections in 1992. Iliescu's party (FSN, then FDSN, then PDSR, and finally PSD) had the upper hand over opposition parties in the first years of the transition by exposing their opponents as allies to the allegedly secessionist Hungarian Alliance (UDMR). However, not all the 'successors' of the PCR joined the FSN. Hardline communists and the hard core nationalist propagandists of Ceauşescu formed their own parties – the Socialist Workers Party (PSM) and the Greater Romania Party (PRM) respectively – and came together as a coalition with the Party of Romanian Social Democracy (PDSR) in 1994–1996. The PSM then merged with the PDSR after 2000 which later became the Social Democratic Party (PSD). The PRM remained a separate entity, providing passive support to all governments during the Iliescu presidencies.

As it took the small anti-communist parties, mostly based on inter-war historical parties, many years to become fully organized, Romania had its first genuine alternation of power only in 1996, when together with the UDMR and PD they managed to secure a majority as the Romanian Democratic Convention (CDR). Despite fears to the contrary, Iliescu left power peacefully and so ended the Romanian political transition. Educated in Moscow in his youth, then marginalized by the West for his initial harsh treatment of political opponents, Iliescu had nevertheless become convinced by 1996 that Romania should join the EU and NATO, and in 1996 he tried to build a national consensus around this idea. When he returned to power in 2000 he wanted European recognition more than anything else, so he asked the UDMR to remain as part of a new government coalition.[4]

The Romanian political transition therefore shares few features with Central Europe. Rather, it followed a different 'Balkan' pattern, which still greatly impacts current Romanian politics, and which has three essential features:

Low political institutionalization. Popular mobilization mattered enormously for achieving Romania's democratization, as alternative elites did not exist, and the commitment of former communists to liberalization was lower than in Central Europe. Once the armed repression ceased, widespread discontent started to manifest itself as open opposition, unorganized and street-based at first, then more and more structured later. Romanians were strongly encouraged and motivated by changes in Central Europe and tried to imitate anti-communist movements in that region. Gradually, a more organized, civilized and peaceful

4   This political history of the transition is based on Mungiu, A. *Românii după '89* (Bucureşti: Humanitas, 1996) and Mungiu-Pippidi, A. 'The Return of Populism. The 2000 Romanian Elections', *Government and Opposition*, 36 (2) 2001, 230–252.

civil society developed. It is the media and the civil society, rather than the parties, which can be found behind the best policies in Romania. Parties have never attained the professionalism of Central European ones, and have never succeeded in providing a good quality of governance, which showed greatly during EU accession negotiations.

Predatory elites in charge. The former communist power establishment was stronger and more determined to protect its advantage in Romania than in Central Europe, where it had less to fear, as the worst of communism could be conveniently blamed on the Soviets. While the PCR itself was more of a loose catch-all structure, networks of real influence linked various sectors of society with the *Securitate*, with the goal of generating profit for themselves. These networks worked hard to save their influence and convert it into wealth, even if that meant sacrificing the PCR itself, and creating an opportunistic replacement. As elections have rarely touched anything other than Parliament and government, these structures of influence within the secret services, military and business (such as banks) retained their power and succeeded in controlling the initial phase of privatization and generating immense wealth for themselves. Romania's much discussed corruption is mostly due to the existence of this 'predatory elite',[5] which engaged in rent-seeking behaviour, practically capturing the state and 'privatizing' government. These groups cannot be described as business oligarchs capturing the state, as the statesmen were also the oligarchs. On the political integrity list published by a Coalition for a Clean Parliament in 2005, several PSD politicians were featured with huge personal fortunes, despite having no registered businesses and having been on the (modest) state payroll for the entirety of Romania's transition.[6] Iliescu's loss of power, both in 1996 and in 2004, despite the absence of a popular challenger was due to the disappointment of blue collar voters with his indulgence towards what was perceived as Romania's corrupt PDSR/PSD oligarchy.

Red-brown alliance strategy. In multiethnic Romania, as well as the rest of the Balkans, the combination of nationalism and socialism proved to have a stronger appeal than socialism alone, providing former communist elites with a remarkable surviving tool. To reinforce their mass appeal, the PCR's successors in Romania turned more and more nationalistic, which proved

---

[5] The term was coined by sociologist Barrington Moore to describe a group of people who in the process of generating wealth for themselves generate large scale poverty for their society. See Moore, B., Jr. *Injustice: The Social Bases of Obedience and Revolt* (White Plains: M.E. Sharpe, 1978).

[6] See Oprea, M. *Mostenitorii securitatii* (Bucureşti: Humanitas, 2004); also Romanian Coalition for a Clean Parliament, *A Quest for Political Integrity* (Iaşi: Polirom, 2005).

to be to their electoral advantage.[7] They also repeatedly allied themselves with chauvinistic right-wing parties. Nationalism decreased after 1996, when a treaty signed with Hungary finally settled Romania's current borders. Due to Romania's EU accession bid, it has also become too politically costly for any party to govern with the chauvinistic PRM, although informal alliances have survived to this day.

SOCIETAL EXPLANATIONS

The answer to the crucial question of 'who governs?' was therefore clear in Romania's transition. Out of the fifteen years of the Romanian political transition, one man, Iliescu, a former communist apparatchik, and the parties he supported have governed for twice as long as their opponents. When governing during the first six years of Romanian's transition, they allowed several former communist organizations to maintain and consolidate their positions. So incomplete was the Romanian victory against such forces that by 2005, the year Romania signed its Accession Treaty with the EU, the army still defended officers who had shot on anti-Ceauşescu protesters and refused to transfer the PCR archives to a civilian authority. The 2004 Regular Report of the European Commission on Romania's progress towards accession also complains of the existence within the Ministry of Justice of a full fledged surveillance service.[8] This service = the Independent Service of Protection and Anti-corruption = is fully staffed by former Securitate officers and was still spying on judges in 2004. It had its powers trimmed only in 2005.

Despite his skilful manipulation of circumstances, Iliescu would never have succeeded in dominating Romania's transition had he not enjoyed popular support. Ten years after his election victory in May 1990, when he gathered 83% of the vote, in the 2000 elections trust in Iliescu still accounted for most of the variance in explanatory models of the vote for the PDSR. The reasons for this tremendous popularity lay behind his successful capitalization on the December 1989 events. His profile as a more moderate and humane Ceauşescu and a 'good' apparatchik was appealing for a population high on residual communist attitudes. By 1999, two-thirds of Romanians still thought that communism had been a good idea badly put into practice, and Ceauşescu was still seen as embodying essential leadership qualities, especially in the countryside.

[7] For an ample discussion on this see Gallagher, T. *Romania after Ceauşescu: The Politics of Intolerance* (Edinburgh: Edinburgh University Press, 1995).
[8] European Commission, *Regular Report on Romania's Progress towards Accession*, COM(2004) 657 final, Brussels, 6 October 2004, p. 21.

The urban-rural divide was especially salient in the first rounds of elections, with cities voting for anti-communists, and peasants for socialists. Romania preserved, due to its historical underdevelopment, the largest share of rural population in Europe (except Moldova and Albania) consisting of subsistence farmers or pensioners from the collective socialist farms. This is a captive constituency for local communist 'gatekeepers', people who control local resources, from firewood to cash subsidies and who have always sided with the FSN and its successors, simply because they do not want a countryside with prosperous and autonomous farmers to emerge. This poor and barely literate part of the population has also found it more natural that a strong leader, rather than Parliament, should make the government.

Some of these attitudes, such as support for freedom versus equality, or for representative democracy versus authoritarianism, have gradually changed over time, with freedom as an overriding value and democracy as the best possible form of government slowly establishing themselves as the norm. The choice between equality and freedom as overriding values, as phrased in the World Values Survey,[9] has predicted fairly well throughout Romania's transition if a person is a democrat or non-democrat, if she votes post-communist or anti-communist, nationalist or pro-European. Collectivism is closely linked with nationalism, ethnocentrism and a vote for post-communist parties in public opinion models. Residual communist attitudes seem to be strongly grounded in persisting institutional arrangements from communist times.[10] Individuals who depend on the state, from workers in state industries to pensioners, especially the poor and less educated, are considerably more collectivist than others. Collectivism is an ideology by default more than choice, since most of those who prefer equality to freedom do not place themselves on the left-right ideological spectrum at all, declaring ideology to be irrelevant to their political choice. Less than a third of Romanian voters use the left-right distinction to ground their electoral choice. For a very long time the strong appeal of Iliescu explained most of the votes on the left. Centre-right voters are more ideological, read more newspapers and are less nationalistic. They are also significantly more pro-European.

Despite the gradual change in political culture and the disastrous economic results of the first ten years of transition – Romania was the only accession country with years of sustained inflation – support for post-communist parties

[9] www.worldvaluessurvey.org.
[10] All models quoted here are reported in Mungiu-Pippidi, A. *Politică după communism* (Bucureşti: Humanitas, 2002) and Mungiu-Pippidi, A. 'Fatalistic Political Cultures Revisited', in Klingemann, H-D. et al (eds), Democracy and *Political Culture in Eastern Europe* (London: Routledge, forthcoming).

Table 2.1: Electoral Fortunes during Romania's Political Transition

Party of Coalition		1992	1996	2000	2004
Total votes cast		10,917,716	12,287,671	10,891,910	10,231,476
FSN, FDSN, PDSR, PSD		3,091,221	2,836,011	4,040,212	3,798,607
PD (originally FSN, then split)		1,133,355	1,617,384	825,437	Part of DA
PUNR (Nationalist)		887,597	518,962	154,761	56,414
CDR	PNT CD	2,204,025	3,772,084	575,706	196,027
(1st anti-communist coalition)	PNL	(below threshold)		(below threshold)	(below threshold)
				814,381	Part of DA
DA ALLIANCE (PNL–PD) (2nd anti-communist coalition)		—	—	—	3,250,663
PRM (Nationalists)		421,042	558,026	2,288,483	1,394,698
PSM		—	—	96,636	—
UDMR		830,195	837,760	751,310	637,109
APR (PDSR splinter)		—	—	465,535	—
Total vote for anti-communists		2,492,891	3,772,084	1,390,087	3,446,690
Total vote for post-communists		5,880,873	5,530,383	8,261,063	5,249,719
Who governed		Post-communists with support from nationalists	Anti-communists with support of UDMR and PID	Post-communists as minority government	Anti-communists in coalition with UDMR

throughout the transition remained higher than support for challenger parties (see Table 2.1). If some political change was achieved, it was due to the shifting alliances among parties, and the mobilization of the small undecided electorate. Had all PCR successor parties ran united in every election, the Romanian anti-communists would have never managed to win. They have never succeeded in getting more than a third of the vote, partly due to their incapacity to penetrate rural areas, partly due to their lack of credible and effective leaders. The first anti-communist President, Emil Constantinescu, who governed from 1996 to 2000, proved mostly a disappointment to voters. He interrupted the tradition of support for Serbia's dictator Slobodan Milošević and backed the West on Kosovo. This might have helped Romania's bid for the EU, but it certainly did not help him with a nationalistic public opinion which sided with the fellow Orthodox Serbs.

THE EUROPEAN FACTOR

Politics changed importantly after Romania applied for EU membership, and furthermore, after it was granted 'candidate' status in 1999. This meant that tutorship from Brussels had become acceptable even for the PDSR, who had spent the first years of transition denying the right of the Council of Europe to intervene in Romania's affairs. It meant that every government had to accept the standards that Iliescu had deliberately criticized at the beginning of transition – when he was a promoter of a Romanian 'original democracy', without political parties. By 1996 the PDSR and its supporters had achieved firm control over many crucial areas, granting tenure in the superior courts to all their people, so they had less to fear than in the early 1990s. Nevertheless, the prospect of accession to the EU opened the door for a new type of political change, a change pushed from below but taking advantage of external conditionality, necessary in a society where powerful people remained above the law. From 1996 on, democratization progressed slowly but irreversibly in nearly every field (see Table 2.2), although overall performance remained below Central European levels.[11] Although Europeanization has remained largely formal and superficial in many areas, in practically every area where the top-down approach only was tried, it worked each time when domestic promoters pushed for it.[12]

---

[11] For an account on the narrowing down of the differences between Romania and Central Europe see Mungiu-Pippidi, A. 'Romania and Poland', in Diamond, L. and Morlino, L. (eds) *Assessing the Quality of Democracy* (Baltimore: Johns Hopkins University Press, 2005), pp. 213–237.

[12] For successes and limits of Romania's Europeanization see Mungiu-Pippidi, A. 'EU Enlargement and Democracy Progress', in Emerson, M. (ed) *Democratization of the European Neighborhood* (Brussels: Centre for European Policy Studies, 2005), pp. 15–37.

Table 2.2: Democratic Evolution after 1997: Freedom House Scores

Freedom House Nations in Transit Democracy Scores (0–7, with 7 the poorest performance)	1997	1998	1999	2001	2002	2003	2004	2005	2006
Electoral Process	3.25	3.25	2.75	3.00	3.00	2.75	2.75	2.75	2.75
Civil Society	3.75	3.75	3.00	3.00	3.00	2.75	2.50	2.25	2.25
Independent Media	4.25	4.00	3.50	3.50	3.50	3.75	3.75	4.00	3.50
Governance	4.25	4.00	3.50	3.75	3.75	3.75	3.75	n/a	n/a
National Democratic Governance	n/a	n/a	n/a	n/a	n/a	n/a	n/a	3.50	3.50
Local Democratic Governance	n/a	n/a	n/a	n/a	n/a	n/a	n/a	3.00	3.00
Judicial Framework and Independence	4.25	4.25	4.25	4.25	4.25	4.25	4.25	4.00	3.75
Corruption	n/a	n/a	4.25	4.50	4.75	4.50	4.50	4.25	4.00

Sources: Freedom House; data gathered from www.freedomhouse.hu

The EU was especially concerned with the state of corruption, a largely misunderstood phenomenon that Brussels thought it could fight by legal prosecution alone. Asking the state captors to fight corruption has predictably brought no positive results, and Romanian's Freedom House corruption scores during the tenure of the last PDSR/PSD government (2000–2004) reflect this adequately.[13] The Transparency International scores for Romania also improved during this period of unprecedented Brussels-driven 'anti-corruption'.[14] The fall from power of the PSD in 2004 was in part due to a domestic anti-corruption campaign and dealt a serious blow to the predatory elite and generated new opportunities to build an economy based on fair competition. While encouraging, there is still much work that remains to be done.

The policy distance between incumbent and challenger elites was initially far greater in Romania than in Central Europe. The more elites agree on essential issues, such as privatization, the smoother and faster the transition from communism to capitalism. In the case of Central Europe there was a consensus for capitalism from the onset of transition, simply because the communist parties there had already exhausted the possibilities of reforming the socialist economy prior to 1989. In Romania, Iliescu tried an in-between approach in the first years of the transition and failed. The attempt only managed to create over one million property-related lawsuits, generate hyperinflation which impoverished millions, prevent the emergence of a land market until 1999, and shape an entrepreneurial class closer to the Russian oligarchic model than the Central European one. Policy changed only after 2000, with the PDSR/PSD agreeing to keep the economy open to competition and foreign investment, in other words, to continue the policy of the previous CDR government (1996–2000).

The obvious failure to create a more equitable social market economy, Iliescu's pet project, was not solely responsible for the PDSR converting to the market. Europe mattered greatly. The public, more than in any Central European country, wanted Romania to join 'Europe' and compared the country's performance with that of the Central European countries. The laggard status with which Romania was labelled throughout most of its transition was bitterly resented and was made a source of constant media criticism. The PDSR/PSD needed the Romanian economy to become successfully integrated with the European one, and after securing their domestic domination, seeking European recognition was their next important objective. Romania's former

[13] See Freedom House, *Nations in Transit 2005: Democratization from Central Europe to Eurasia* (Boulder Co.: Rowman and Littlefield, 2005). Also: www.freedomhouse.hu/nitransit/2005/romania.pdf.
[14] Compare the annual reports available at www.transparency.org/publications/annual_report.

communists have been genuinely convinced of the EU and its advantages. Political parties started being concerned with linking to the party groups in the European Parliament. Even the PRM sought to change from an anti-Semitic party to an acceptable European one.

The existence of a European option prevented Romania from staying as Albania or regressing to become a new Belarus. The incentive of European integration lured even the successors of communism and encouraged the pro-change constituency. Every step of the Romanian political transition, as Freedom House reports show,[15] had to be fought over fiercely, and there is still a way to go for Romania to achieve a substantial democracy. But more than any constitution or electoral law, European integration and the prospect of accession to the EU have shaped Romanian politics, and it is in this challenging environment that Europe achieved its largest success to-date. Romania's transition may have seemed long and strenuous for Romanians, but from Ceauşescu's snipers and Iliescu's vigilante miners to the signing of the Accession Treaty with the EU has taken only fifteen years.

[15] Freedom House, op cit.

CHAPTER THREE

The Romanian Economy since 1989

Alan Smith

Romania has experienced the greatest difficulty in creating the institutions of a market economy of the ten former Central and Eastern European (CEE) countries that were invited to open negotiations for accession to the European Union (EU) in the 1990s. As a result it was the last of them to be awarded the status of a functioning market economy by the European Commission in October 2004. Romania arguably inherited the worst starting conditions for implementing the transition to a market economy outside the former Soviet Union. The Ceauşescu government had borrowed heavily from western banks between 1967 and 1980 to finance investment in engineering industries, refineries and petrochemical plants and a number of grandiose construction projects including the Danube-Black Sea canal and the construction of the House of the People in Bucharest, while neglecting the production of consumer goods. These investments necessitated further imports of crude oil, raw material and components that could not be produced domestically to maintain production. The failure to generate hard currency exports to service the debt and to maintain essential imports culminated in a financial crisis in 1981 which necessitated the rescheduling of debt. Ceauşescu then embarked on a policy of rapid debt repayment which could only be achieved by draconian cuts in imports of energy, consumer goods and equipment. As a result, by 1989 the economy was on the verge of collapse, with widespread shortages and severe rationing of energy, while the population had endured nearly a decade of deep austerity and the capital stock had become increasingly obsolete.

The slow pace of the transition to a market economy can only be attributed in part to the adverse economic circumstances facing the country in 1989. As this chapter shows, it largely reflects the reluctance of the left-of-centre governments that ruled Romania for eleven of the fifteen years between

December 1989 and the end of 2004 to implement the structural changes that were required to attract foreign investment and to create a modern open market economy that was capable of responding to the demands of consumers inside and outside the country. This was reinforced by the failure of the right-of-centre government that ruled from the end of 1996 to 2000 to implement a coherent and co-ordinated reform strategy.

1990–2004 – An Overview

For much of the period, the Romanian economy has been something of a hybrid: neither fully marketized nor centrally planned. The industrial sector was largely composed of inefficient and over-staffed large- and medium-scale enterprises inherited from the communist era that continued to produce relatively obsolete metallurgical and engineering products and survived largely by means of government subsidies, 'soft' credits from state-owned banks and arrears to the state budget and to other enterprises, notably utilities and energy producers. Large-scale enterprises that were profitable (largely in the energy and resource extraction sectors) were used as sources of hidden subsidies for non-viable sectors as well as a source of private income for 'insiders'. Utilities (electricity and gas distribution, railways and urban transport) remained under state control and suffered from lack of investment and modernisation and of over-staffing and made considerable losses. The market sector largely consisted of a small, under-capitalised small business sector, a flourishing 'grey' economy and a small-scale agricultural sector which employed over 30% of the labour force, but contributed to only 13–14% of gross domestic product (GDP). The failure to reform the banking and financial system – which has been wracked by financial scandals that have resulted in the loss of life-savings for many citizens – meant that it was incapable of providing adequate mediation between savers and borrowers. Moreover, the small enterprise sector has largely had to rely on self-financing for investment, thus hindering its development. The major sources of external income have come from the labour-intensive, clothing and textile industries which largely rely on outward-processing contracts and remittances from approximately two million workers abroad. The narrow production base inherited from the communist era and the slow pace of restructuring means that Romania remains dependent on imports for machinery and equipment, a wide range of consumer goods, energy and raw materials.

The slow pace of structural reform, involving continued state subsidies to industry and enterprise arrears to the budget, has also made it difficult to bring about fiscal balance. As a result governments have struggled to restrict budget deficits which have largely been monetized, resulting in high rates of inflation.

Much of the impetus for reform has resulted from pressures by external agencies, including the EU, the International Monetary Fund (IMF) and the World Bank. Over the period, Romania signed six standby agreements with the IMF which stipulated macroeconomic targets and structural reforms but only successfully completed one in 2003. Nevertheless, some progress has been made, particularly since 2000. After experiencing major falls in industrial output in 1990–1992 and in 1997–1999, Romania has experienced strong growth from 2000 onwards. Although privatisation has been slow, the private sector accounted for 70% of GDP in 2004 as privatisation accelerated in 2003–2004, with an increasing number of direct sales of enterprises and financial institutions to largely foreign owners who are investing in modernising plant and equipment. There are some indications that Romania is finally moving up the export 'product ladder' and limiting its dependence on labour-intensive and resource-intensive exports, with increasing exports of machinery and electrical equipment, including components for the A-380 airbus, and automobiles. The telecommunications and information technology sectors have been opened up to competition and have expanded in the early 2000s with internet penetration increasing rapidly while most large towns can now boast some modern shopping malls and out-of-town supermarkets. Reforms to the financial sector and the development of new financial instruments are beginning to take effect and are leading to the development of a young professional, consumption-oriented, middle class. However, levels of poverty remain high by West European standards and will complicate the process of accession to the EU. The broad parameters of economic development in the period covered by this chapter are shown in Table 1.

ECONOMIC POLICY AND PERFORMANCE FROM 1990–1996

The period between 1990 and 1996 covers the first period of government by the left of centre National Salvation Front (NSF) and its successor, the Party of Social Democracy of Romania (PDSR). The first post-communist Prime Minister, Petre Roman, attempted to implement structural reforms intended to introduce a market economy within a two-year period in the summer of 1990. However, these proposals resulted in major falls in real wages and consumption in 1991 and were opposed by vested interests inside and outside the government culminating in the overthrow of the Roman government following the storming of government offices by miners in September 1991. Roman's successors, Teodor Stolojan and Nicolae Văcăroiu, wary of public hostility to radical reform, both pursued gradualist reforms involving the phased removal of price controls, a largely ineffective voucher system of

Table 3.1: Basic Parameters of Romanian Economic Performance by Political
Periods

	1990-92	1993-96	1997-2000	2001-04
Cumulative over the period				
GDP growth	-25.1%	17.6%	-12.5%	25.3%
Industrial output growth	-54.0%	24.0%	-23.0%	28.0%
Net average real wage growth	-22.6%	8.3%	-15.4%	31.6%
Current account balance	-$5,772m	-$6,045m	-$7,697m	-$13,322m
Foreign direct investment	$92m	$1,118m	$5,422m	$9,534m
End of Period				
Poverty (population)	=	20.1%	35.9%	25.1%*
External Debt	$3.2m	$8.3m	$10.6m	$26.8m
Annual Inflation end-year**	199.2%	56.9%	40.7%	9.3%
Income per capita (ppp)	$3,542	$4,591	$5,660	$7,883
Registered unemployment	8.2	6.6	10.5	6.2

Notes: * = 2003; ** = End-year inflation rate for last year in period
Sources. Authors estimates from data in: Comisia Anti-Sărăciei si Promovare a
Incluziunii Sociale, *Dinamica sărăciei și a sărăciei severe în perioada 1995-2003*
(Bucharest: Comisia Anti-Sărăcie si Promovare a Incluziunii Sociale, 2005)
(www.caspis.ro); Economist Intelligence Unit, *Country Report on Romania* (London:
Economist Intelligence Unit, various issues); European Bank for Reconstruction and
Development, *Transition Reports* (London: European Bank for Reconstruction and
Development, various years); Eurostat; National Bank of Romania, *Annual,
Quarterly and Monthly Bulletins* (National Bank of Romania: Bucharest, various
years); National Institute of Statistics, Bucharest (www.insse.ro); Organization for
Economic Cooperation and Development; *Romanian Business Journal* (Bucharest,
various issues)

privatisation, minor structural reforms and the continued subsidisation of heavy
industry. No serious attempt was made to reform the financial sector, although
a few foreign banks were allowed to undertake some limited operations. The
failure to bring about macroeconomic stabilisation resulted in year-end rates
of inflation of 223% and 199% in 1991 and 1992 respectively and a current
account deficit of 8% of GDP in 1992. Despite the gradual pace of reform and
attempts to shield the population from economic realities, Romania experienced the severest 'transition recession' of the non-Soviet former communist
economies with industrial output falling by 54% and GDP by 25.1% between
1990 and 1992 while unemployment rose from virtually zero to 8.2% by the
end of 1992. An attempt to bring about macroeconomic stabilisation involving
tighter fiscal and monetary policies and the liberalisation of the foreign

THE ROMANIAN ECONOMY   33

exchange market with a single unified exchange rate was introduced in 1993. The strategy contributed to a minor recovery in 1993–1994, with GDP growing by 1.5% and 3.9% respectively. End-year inflation was brought down to 61.7% in 1994 and the current account deficit was reduced to 1.4% of GDP. However, the government embarked on an over-rapid expansion of aggregate demand in 1995–1996 in the run up to parliamentary and presidential elections in 1996. The failure to implement any serious structural reforms and to attract any significant foreign direct investment between 1990 and 1994 meant that this largely resulted in an increase in imports and the resurgence of inflationary pressures. The government attempted to suppress these by imposing price controls over state-owned industry and imposing constraints over the domestic foreign exchange market. Despite these problems the economy staged a minor recovery in 1993–1996 with GDP growing by 17.6% and industrial output by 24%.

1996–2000: 'SHOCK, BUT NO THERAPY' REFORMS

The second distinct economic phase covers the administration of the centre-right coalition government of the Romanian Democratic Convention (CDR) from 1997 to 2000. The CDR government, headed initially by Victor Ciorbea, attempted to introduce a strategy for the rapid introduction of a market economy, under the guidance of the IMF which was largely modelled on the Polish 'shock therapy' reforms introduced in 1990. This involved price liberalisation and an attempt to align domestic prices with world market prices, the removal of subsidies to loss-making enterprises and public utilities and subsidies on consumer goods and services including food and energy, the abolition of import controls and the introduction of a single market-determined exchange rate involving an initial sharp devaluation of the leu. However, even the published programme contained contradictions, indicating disagreements within the coalition which were to make much of the programme inoperative. The government also proposed to accelerate structural reforms by privatising large- and medium-scale state-owned enterprises and banks and by restructuring loss-making public utilities and energy producers. The restructuring of loss-making industries and utilities prior to privatisation involved the closure of loss-making mines and cuts in capacity and major redundancies in the metallurgical, engineering and petrochemical industries. The liberalisation of prices and foreign exchange markets resulted in an immediate surge in open inflation with consumer prices rising by 155% in 1997 while wages rose by 90% resulting in a fall in real wages of 25%. Although year-end inflation was reduced to 41% in 1998, no further progress was made in reducing inflation by the end of 2000. Attempts to restructure loss-making enterprises contributed to a second 'transition recession' with GDP falling by 18.4% and industrial output by 34% between 1997 and 2000. Registered unemployment rose to 11.8% by the end of 1999.

However proposals for accelerated privatisation and industrial restructuring fell badly behind schedule in 1997 as a result of a combination of disagreements within the governing coalition and resistance by the state bureaucracy and the trade unions. Ciorbea was replaced as prime minister in April 1998 by Radu Vasile who drafted a new set of proposals to accelerate privatisation and implement structural reform. These met resistance, sometimes violent, from the trade unions and there was widespread civil unrest. Vasile was replaced as prime minister in December 1999 by the governor of the National Bank, Mugur Isărescu, who succeeded in halting the fall in GDP and industrial output in 2000. Although 1997–2000 saw some successes in privatising the telecommunications sector and some state-owned banks, only 60% of GDP was produced by the private sector in 2000 and over half of capital remained in state hands.

2001–2004: ACCELERATED, BUT GRADUALIST, REFORMS

Elections in December 2000 brought the return of a minority government, headed by the PDSR – which was renamed the Social Democratic Party (PSD) in 2001 – under the leadership of Adrian Năstase who represented the modernising wing of the party. The government recognised that the achievement of its major foreign policy goals – membership of NATO and above all the EU – would require the creation of a functioning market economy. The government also recognised that macroeconomic stabilisation and sustained economic growth would be impossible without deeper structural reforms and embarked on programmes agreed with the IMF and the EU to implement the latter. The government negotiated an eighteen-month 'standby' agreement with the IMF in October 2001, which it successfully completed in 2003 after some extensions and waivers for failing to implement privatisation targets in the financial and energy sectors. This was the first standby agreement to be completed following five failures in the 1990s. Structural reforms included the restructuring and privatisation, or closure, of large loss-making enterprises in the engineering sector, particularly those responsible for arrears to the state budget; reforms to the energy sector to bring prices in line with world market prices and to eliminate losses prior to privatisation; the privatisation of utilities in gas and electricity distribution; and the closure of more loss-making mines; reductions in the public sector workforce and controls over public sector wages and the privatisation of remaining state-owned banks.

Nevertheless, progress in privatisation, which increasingly involved the sale of majority shares in enterprises and banks to foreign strategic investors, sometimes for symbolic sums in exchange for commitments to invest in the plant and to retain large proportions of the workforce, frequently fell behind schedule and invoked criticism from the IMF and the World Bank. The pace of privatisation accelerated in 2003–2004 and included the largest privatisation in Romania's history with the sale a majority share in the integrated oil company Petrom to OMV of Austria in July 2004 for a sum which will amount to €1.39 billion to 1.53 billion after OMV has invested in modernisation and restructuring refineries and pipelines.

The PSD government also started to implement, following prompting from the EU and the IMF, the sale of gas and electricity distributors to foreign companies. By the end of 2004 large sections of the telecommunications and information technology sector, the banking sector, the pharmaceutical industry, the metallurgical industry, the automotive industry, the brewing industry and the tobacco industry had been privatised, or part-privatised, and were being reconstructed by the new owners. Investment in industrial modernisation and in a number of large-scale infrastructure projects, including motorways, a second unit at the Cernavoda nuclear power station, tourist facilities and the construction of out-of-town shopping centres has been a major factor contributing to a resurgence of economic growth in 2001–2004, with GDP growing by over 25% and industrial output, including construction, by 28%.

IMF agreements also included policies for the progressive reduction of inflation involving reductions in budget deficits and stricter monetary policies. These have met with partial success in that the rate of inflation was reduced annually and fell to 9.3% in 2004, the first time it has fallen below 10% since the lifting of communist price controls. However, an expansion of aggregate demand in 2003–2004, caused by a rapid expansion of real wages and consumer credit, has continued to suck in imports, resulting in a current account deficit of US$ 5.9 billion, equivalent to 8.3% of GDP in 2004. However, Romania's ability to attract foreign investment, improved credit ratings and high levels of foreign exchange reserves means that deficits of this size can be adequately financed, although they indicate that further structural reforms will be required for the Romanian economy to withstand competitive pressures in the enlarged EU. Although the EU finally recognised Romania as having a 'functioning market economy' in October 2004, it raised major concerns about widespread corruption and the lack of independence of the judiciary and its ability to enforce property rights and provide equal treatment to foreign investors which impacted negatively on the business environment.

The elections of December 2004 resulted in a further change in government with the replacement of the PSD government by the Justice and Truth alliance (DA) headed by Călin Popescu-Tăriceanu. The DA's economic policies are based on market-liberalism and included the imposition of a flat-rate income and corporation tax at 16% and attempts to amend the Labour Code, which was seen as too employee-friendly. The DA government has pledged to accelerate structural reforms including the privatisation of remaining state-owned energy distributors and banks and the liquidation of loss-making enterprises. However, the IMF, which approved a two-year 'precautionary standby agreement' in July 2004, which allows it to monitor Romania's economic performance in the run up to EU accession, has expressed concerns that its taxation and expenditure proposals threaten to aggravate the delicate macroeconomic situation and is seeking further reductions in fiscal deficits.

THE COSTS OF TRANSITION: POVERTY AND UNEMPLOYMENT

Although the transition to a market economy has been gradual, it has been accompanied by increased poverty and in some cases deep poverty. Although unemployment fell in the period 2000–2004, there are pockets of high long-term unemployment, particularly in the northeast of the country and in other areas that have been affected by enterprise closures. Unemployment remains low in the north-western counties bordering Hungary and the Municipality of Bucharest. A report by the Commission for Anti-Poverty and Promotion of Social Inclusion (CASPIS) which measures poverty using a standardised methodology designed by the World Bank and comparing household per capita income with the cost of a minimum subsistence basket, shows that poverty grew from 20.1% of the population in 1996 to 35.9% in 2000, but then fell back to 25.1% in 2003.[1] The proportion of the population living in deep poverty grew from 6.3% in 1996 to 13.8% at the end of 2000 as GDP contracted, before falling to 8.6% in 2003 as GDP rose. Poverty is greatest amongst the Roma population, where the incidence was as high as 76.8% in 2003 and lowest amongst the Hungarian population, where the incidence was 14.9%. In the same year, 38% of the rural of the rural population were in poverty compared with 13.8% of the urban population, with 13.9% and 3.8% respectively living in deep poverty. The incidence of poverty is inversely related to the level of education and is highest in families with three, or more children.

[1]   Comisia Anti-Sărăciei si Promovare a Incluziunii Sociale, *Dinamica sărăciei și a sărăciei severe în perioada 1995–2003* (Bucharest: Comisia Anti-Sărăciei si Promovare a Incluziunii Sociale, 2005) (www.caspis.ro).

CONCLUSION

Progress towards the development of a functioning market economy in Romania has arguably been the slowest of all of the ten states to sign an accession treaty with the EU. This has reflected a combination of difficult initial circumstances, political inertia, rejection and sabotage of reform policies by an entrenched bureaucracy which in many cases has survived from the communist era and the inability of reform-minded politicians on the centre-right and centre-left to agree on a programme of reforms. Reforms accelerated between 2000 and 2004 under pressures from the IMF, the World Bank and the EU resulting in an acceleration of privatisation and the progressive reduction in inflation. Nevertheless, reform implementation remained slow by the standards of other accession economies. The formation of a centre-right administration since the end of 2004 has contributed to an acceleration of reforms including the introduction of flat-rate income and profits taxes and the liberalisation of capital flows but the relaxation of macroeconomic policies has aggravated macroeconomic imbalances.

CHAPTER FOUR

Romania and Euro-Atlantic Integration

David Phinnemore

When Romania joins the European Union (EU) in 2007 – or 2008 – an historic milestone in its post-communist history will have been passed. Not only will it have achieved the cherished goal of entry into the EU but it will now be a member of all the major organizations of the wide ranging, overlapping and interlocking processes that constitute Euro-Atlantic integration. It will be a member of the EU, of the North Atlantic Treaty Organization (NATO) and of the Council of Europe. Fears of being excluded, of being marginalized from the European mainstream, of being condemned to an uncertain future in some grey zone between a European core, a Russia-dominated east and the fringes of Asia – fears that have resonated in political and media discourse over Romania's future since 1989 – will have been confounded. Romania, having gained membership of the Council of Europe in 1993, of NATO in 2003 will now be a full participant in Euro-Atlantic integration processes.

THE EARLY 1990s: A STRUGGLE FOR ACCEPTANCE

Looking back at the early 1990s, however, it was far from certain that Romania would reach such a position. Although the country had been courted by the West during the 1970s and had established contractual relations with the then European Economic Community – an agreement on trade in industrial goods was concluded in 1980 – its international standing in the late 1980s and in the years immediately following the overthrow of Ceauşescu was far from enviable. Concerns over the human rights situation in the country and in particular the treatment of ethnic Hungarians led to much international criticism of the Ceauşescu regime. This was followed in 1990 by doubts about the commitment of the ruling National Salvation Front (FSN) and Romania's new president, Ion Iliescu, to democracy, the rule of law, and respect for human and minority rights, particular in the light of the violent events in Târgu Mureş in March and the government-backed descent of the miners on Bucharest to quash anti-government demonstrations in June. Such developments were roundly condemned by the European Community (EC), NATO and the Council of Europe. The EC delayed both Romania's inclusion in the PHARE programme and the conclusion of an agreement on trade and commercial and economic cooperation until later in 1990. Any hopes that Romania might have entertained of being among the first of the Central and Eastern European (CEE) countries to negotiate a Europe Agreement = the EC's initial response to the CEE countries' desire for closer relations and ultimately membership = were also dashed, particularly given additional concerns about the new government's commitment to and progress with economic reform. The events of 1990 also raised concerns in the Council of Europe about admitting Romania.

Doubts about commitments to economic and political reform = prerequisites for progressing with Euro-Atlantic integration = persisted into 1991 and beyond. A second visit to Bucharest by the Jiu Valley miners in September 1991 and the forced resignation of Petre Roman as Prime Minister did little to improve the situation. Nevertheless, formally at least, Iliescu and the government were committed to Romania's 'return to Europe' and integration with and into the key organizations. As much was signalled to NATO in an invitation to its Secretary-General, Manfred Wörner, to pay an official visit to Bucharest in 1990 and in a formal application for membership three years later. A desire for integration with the EC was also evident and was formally expressed in a request in March 1991 for negotiations on a Europe Agreement to be opened. Efforts to gain entry into the Council of Europe were pursued too, albeit with only limited success, due in part to a concerted campaign by Hungary, which gained membership in November 1990, to block Romania's entry until concerns over the position of the Hungarian minority in the country had been satisfactorily addressed.

While progress was slow in achieving integration, the pace quickened in 1992–1994. Not only was a Europe Agreement concluded with the EC (1 February 1993), but Romania also gained membership of the Council of Europe (7 October 1993) and became the first CEE country to sign a Partnership for Peace (PfP) with NATO (26 January 1994). Whereas the Europe Agreement provided for free trade in industrial goods, political dialogue and cooperation with the EC in a wide variety of areas,[1] Council of Europe membership

[1] *Europe Agreement establishing an association between the European Communities and their Member States, of the one part, and Romania, of the other part,* Official Journal of the European Communities, L357, 31 December 1994.

signalled acceptance by European countries of Romania's commitment to uphold democratic principles as well as the European Convention on Human Rights. The PfP, derided by its critics as a 'partnership for procrastination', was nevertheless viewed optimistically as a first step towards possible NATO membership. Its emphasis was on defence-related cooperation including joint operations between Romania and NATO.

In the Queue for EU and NATO Membership

By now both NATO and the EU were now beginning to consider how and when to admit CEE countries. The announcement by the European Council in June 1993 in Copenhagen that 'those associated countries of Central and Eastern Europe that so desire shall become members' was warmly received in Romania which by now was becoming viewed as a 'laggard' in terms of both economic and political transition and European integration. The Visegrad countries = the Czech Republic, Hungary, Poland and Slovakia = were making noticeably more progress on each front and it soon became clear that the other 'new' CEE countries = Estonia, Latvia, Lithuania and Slovenia = were overtaking Romania, at least as far as their prospects for integration with the EU were concerned. Romania may have seen its Europe Agreement enter into force in early 1995, drawn up a national strategy for preparing Romania for accession to the EU, and submitted a formal application for EU membership on 22 June 1995, but within two years it was evident that others would be entering both NATO and the EU before it. This was despite the new optimism created by the success of the more reform-oriented Romanian Democratic Convention (CDR) in the 1996 elections.

The CDR promised much and this was recognised by EU and NATO leaders in the decisions they took in 1997 concerning enlargement even though neither organization invited Romania to open accession negotiations. NATO leaders in July 1997 issued only three membership invitations: to the Czech Republic, Hungary and Poland. But they did make a commitment to invite more states to join the Atlantic Alliance and recognized 'with great interest . . . the positive developments towards democracy and the rule of law in . . . especially Romania'.[2] This was taken to mean that Romania = along with Slovenia = was next in line for membership, with an invitation coming possibly as soon as 1999. Equally encouraging was the decision of the European Council in Luxembourg in December 1997 to include Romania in the EU's accession

---

[2]   NATO, *Madrid Declaration on Euro-Atlantic Security and Cooperation*, Madrid, 8 July 1997, point 8

process to be launched in March 1998, even if the country was not invited to open accession negotiations alongside Cyprus, the Czech Republic, Estonia, Hungary, Poland and Slovenia. Earlier in 1997, in July, the European Commission had issued its opinion on Romania's application for membership. Although it had noted that 'Romania is on its way to satisfy the political criteria' for membership, its overall assessment was less favourable and hence Romania was not recommended for accession negotiations. Romania's progress in creating a market economy may have been deemed to have been 'considerable', but it was equally clear that the country 'would face serious difficulties to cope with the competitive pressure and market forces within the Union in the medium-term'.[3]

The Luxembourg European Council's announcement that Romania, along with the other CEE countries, was 'destined to join' the EU and its decision to launch an 'evolutive and inclusive' accession process provided a major fillip for Romania in realising its goal of full participation in the process of European integration. Rather than pursuing a highly differentiated approach to enlargement with states being either 'ins' or 'outs', involving all in a single process meant that the talk was more of 'ins' and 'pre-ins'. Moreover, concrete steps promoting integration were taken in the course of 1998. Not only did the EU launch its accession process, but an 'enhanced pre-accession strategy' was put in place. This involved increased PHARE assistance, the conclusion of an Accession Partnership identifying short-, medium- and long-term preparations for membership, and an annual review of progress in meeting the criteria for membership. Domestically, the Romanian government was also making efforts to prepare the country for eventual EU membership. A first Minister-Delegate for European Integration had been appointed by the CDR government to coordinate preparations and work had begun on a National Programme for the Adoption of the Acquis.

Achieving progress in meeting the criteria for EU membership proved difficult, particularly given the fractious nature of the CDR and the instability of successive governments in 1996–2000. And this was reflected in the European Commission's 1998 and 1999 reports on Romania's preparedness for membership. Although encouraging developments were acknowledged, the first noted that reforms had been 'far too hesitant and slow' and Romania had made 'very little progress in the creation of a market economy and its capacity to cope with competitive pressure and market forces has worsened'. The assessment of the political situation in Romania was not particularly encouraging

[3] European Commission, *Commission Opinion on Romania's Application for Membership of the European Union*, DOC/97/18, Brussels, 15 July 1997, Conclusion

either. Concerns were expressed about levels of corruption, the treatment of the Roma and the need for reform of the public administration.[4] A year later, the European Commission reported that 'the economic situation in Romania is very worrying and sustained efforts will be needed to put a functioning market economy in place . . . Romania [does] not meet either economic criterion. Regrettably, the situation in Romania has, at best, stabilised compared with last year'.[5] Such reports did not bode well and tended to confirm Romania's position as one of the laggards – along with Bulgaria – in the accession process.

The reports did little too to enhance either the domestic or international standing of the CDR government. They also exacerbated fears that Romania was contributing to its own marginalization within the process of Euro-Atlantic integration. Such fears were rife in Romania in 1999 and were exacerbated by the fact that NATO membership appeared to be no closer than in 1997. Despite Romania's enthusiastic implementation of its PfP, its participation in a range of NATO-led activities, and unwavering support for the West over Kosovo, NATO leaders at their Washington Summit in April 1999 conspicuously failed to invite Romania to join. Frustration led to accusations of 'indifference' towards Romania being levelled against the West by the Romanian President, Emil Constantinescu who had already expressed fears that Romania was being consigned to some South East European 'grey zone'.[6]

DOORS BEGIN TO OPEN WIDE

In fact, 1999 turned out to be a turning point in Romania's quest for entry into NATO and the EU. NATO leaders in Washington were not abandoning enlargement, but rather postponing any new membership invitations until after the Kosovo conflict. This was explicit in the launching of Membership Action Plans (MAP). These were designed to move relations with would-be members beyond PfP and towards membership through improved inter-operability of their forces with those of NATO and the development of military capabilities. To this end Annual National Plans (ANP) would be drawn up and a joint feedback and assessment mechanism established on performance in

4   European Commission, *Regular Report on Progress towards Accession: Romania*, Brussels, 4 November 1998
5   European Commission, *Commission sets out an ambitious accession strategy and proposes to open accession negotiations with six more candidate countries*, IP/99/751, Brussels, 13 October 1999.
6   Phinnemore, D. 'Stuck in the 'Grey Zone'? – Fears and Frustrations in Romania's Quest for EU Membership', *Perspectives on European Politics and Society*, 1 (1) 2000, 95–122.

meeting MAP goals.[7] Moreover, NATO leaders committed themselves to maintaining an 'open door' approach to enlargement, indicating that they expected to issue further membership invitations 'in coming years'.[8] Despite the frustration at not receiving an invitation to join, such developments were welcomed in Romania and the MAP and ANP eagerly pursued.

Equally welcomed was the EU's re-assessment, in the light of the Kosovo conflict, of the strategic value of enlargement in promoting security and stability in Europe. This led the European Commission, despite its critical regular report on Romania in October 1999, to advocate the opening of accession negotiations as part of its call for 'resolute and courageous action' with regard to enlargement.[9] There were provisos, however. Romania would have to reform the organization of and provide more financial resources for childcare institutions and adopt 'appropriate measures' to address the macro-economic situation in the country. Once it was clear that efforts were being made to address these issues, the recommendation to open negotiations was taken up by the Helsinki European Council in December 1999 which also conferred on Romania – as well as all other applicants – the status of 'candidate'. Accession negotiations were formally opened on 15 February 2000. A key milestone had been passed on the road to membership of the EU.

Progress in the negotiations was soon being made. By the end of the 2000, nine of the 31 chapters had been opened and six closed. A further eight chapters were opened in 2001, although by now it was clear that Romania – along with Bulgaria – was trailing behind those that had started negotiations at the same time and would not be involved in a 'big bang' enlargement of the EU to include ten new members. This was planned for 2004. There were also concerns that progress in implementing the necessary domestic reforms to meet the accession criteria could seriously delay accession and there was even talk of Romania actually being overtaken by Croatia in gaining membership. The arrival of a new Romanian government in late 2001 helped ensure that this did not happen.

The Party of Romanian Social Democracy (PDSR) – the principle descendant of the original FSN – had come to power with Iliescu once again as President. Its commitment to Euro-Atlantic integration, doubted on many occasions in the past, had become as strong as that of the ousted CDR and among the first moves of the new Prime Minister, Adrian Năstase, on taking office was the

[7] Watts, L.L. (ed) *Romanian Military Reform and NATO Integration* (Iaşi: The Center for Romanian Studies, 2002).

[8] NATO, *The Alliance's Strategic Concept*, Washington D.C., 23–24 April 1999, point 39.

[9] European Commission, *Composite Paper: Reports on progress towards accession of each of the candidate countries*, Brussels, 13 October 1999, p. 4.

establishment of a dedicated Minster and Ministry of European Integration. This facilitated an intensification of domestic preparations for accession and helped ensure progress in the accession negotiations. By the end of 2002 more than half (16) of the negotiating chapters had been concluded. Assuming the momentum could be maintained, the PDSR = soon to rename itself the Party of Social Democracy (PSD) = would remain on course to oversee the completion of negotiations in 2004. This would allow EU membership to be achieved in 2007, the goal set by the previous government. It would also coincide with parliamentary and presidential elections.

The apparent enthusiasm of the PDSR/PSD for Euro-Atlantic integration was also evident in the way in which it maintained efforts focused on gaining entry into NATO and seeking the support for its accession from key member states. Particular attention was paid to implementing the necessary military reforms identified under the MAP and on ensuring the support of the United States which had launched a 'Strategic Partnership' with Romania in 1997. The new government was eager to maximise the benefits from this. It was also keen to ally Romania with the United States in the wake of 11 September 2001. Parliament decided shortly after the attacks on New York and Washington DC that Romania would participate as a *de facto* NATO ally in actions designed to counter international terrorism. To this end, it agreed to respond positively to any NATO requests for access to airspace, airports and land and sea facilities. Subsequently it would participate in a range of NATO activities. It would also ally itself closely with the United States over Afghanistan and Iraq and in its 'war on terror' more generally. Indeed, Romania's closeness to the United States at times raised concerns within the EU about the country's foreign policy priorities. Considerable concerns were voiced in EU circles at the haste with which the Romanian government in 2002 responded positively to a US request not to handover US citizens to the International Criminal Court. Romanian support for the US was, however, obviously welcomed in the White House and Pentagon which had come to view Romania = given its geo-strategic location and willingness to provide bases and other support = as an increasingly important ally.

ACCESSION TO NATO AND PROGRESS TOWARDS EU MEMBERSHIP

All this helped enhance Romania's case for NATO = and indeed EU = membership.[10] Hence, when the enlargement issue returned to NATO's agenda

---

[10] See Gallagher, T. *Theft of a Nation: Romania since Communist* (London: Hurst, 2004), pp. 324–327.

in 2002 there was little doubt that Romania would be issued with an invitation to join. In fact Romania had only to wait until the Prague Summit of NATO leaders in November 2002 to receive its invitation. Accession negotiations began the following month and were completed in time for the agreed Accession Protocol to be sign on 26 March 2003. Ratification followed and on 29 March 2004, a month earlier than planned, Romania, along with six other CEE countries – Bulgaria, Estonia, Latvia, Lithuania, Slovakia and Slovenia – acceded to NATO. Four days later, the flags of these countries were raised alongside those of the other members at NATO headquarters in Brussels.

With NATO membership achieved the missing piece in Romania's Euro-Atlantic integration jigsaw puzzle was membership of the EU. At the time of its accession to NATO, Romania was still negotiating with the EU. Although 22 of the 31 negotiation chapters had been closed, the financial framework for the accession of Romania and Bulgaria agreed and the Accession Partnership revised, there was still a degree of uncertainty as to whether Romania would accede to the EU as planned in 2007. Major obstacles included the state of the economy and the public administration's capacity to ensure that Romania could meet its obligations as a member of the EU. Moreover, the resignation in October 2003 of the country's Minister of European Integration, Hildegaard Puwak, following allegations that she had channelled EU funds to companies run by her husband and son – Puwak was subsequently cleared – merely added to concerns about the extent of corruption. On the economy too there were concerns. The European Commission had still to declare unequivocally that Romania was a functioning market economy. In its 2003 report, it could only clumsily conclude that 'Romania can be considered as a functioning market economy once the good progress made has continued decisively'.[11] This raised doubts, despite the existence of a Road Map for membership, whether the goal of concluding the accession negotiations before the end of 2004 would be met. Nine difficult chapters remained open. Moreover, the EP was becoming more vocal in highlighting shortcomings in Romania's preparations for membership. In particular there were calls for more to be done to address corruption, ensure the independence of the judiciary, guarantee the freedom of the media, improve the situation of orphans and other children in institutional care homes and transpose and implement the *acquis*.[12]

---

[11] European Commission, 2003 *Regular Report on Romania's progress towards accession*, Brussels, 5 November 2003, p. 121.

[12] European Parliament, *Report on Romania's Progress towards accession*, European Parliament Session Document, A5–0103/004 Final, 24 February 2004 (Rapporteur: Baroness Nicholson of Winterbourne).

Despite such concerns it was clear that the political will existed within the EU for Romania to join the EU. The participation of representatives of the Romanian government and parliament in the European Convention that drafted the EU's Constitutional Treaty in 2002–2003 and in the subsequent IGC signalled the expectation that Romania would soon be joining in the EU. Indeed a date had already been agreed in December 2002 when the accession negotiations with the other CEE countries plus Cyprus and Malta had been concluded. In a 'One Europe' statement the EU's existing member states and the ten countries that had just concluded their negotiations declared their 'full support for the continuous, inclusive and irreversible enlargement process'.[13] The stated objective was to admit Bulgaria and Romania in 2007. Moreover, the EU became increasingly proactive in providing guidance beyond the Accession Partnership and the Road Map on what needed to be done to conclude negotiations as planned. Early in 2004, for example, European Commission officials were instrumental in getting the Romanian government to publish a high profile 'to do' list to reassure the EU that key reforms would be implemented.

EU MEMBERSHIP BECKONS: 2007 OR 2008?

This commitment helped maintain some momentum in the accession negotiations and became particularly important as voices concerned about Romania's readiness for and ability to assume all the obligations of EU membership grew louder. Particular concern was expressed about the country's administrative capacity to ensure effective implementation of and compliance with the *acquis*. Doubts were also being raised about corruption levels in Romania and the government's slow progress in implementing anti-corruption measures. Unsurprisingly this made conclusion of the remaining chapters in 2004 particularly tough. It also meant that negotiations with Bulgaria were concluded – in June 2004 – ahead of those with Romania, raising the possibility of the two countries being decoupled and Romania's accession to the EU being delayed beyond 2007. In the end, the negotiations were concluded in December 2004, but only after the EU's member states had placed considerable pressure to conclude on a European Commission reluctant to do so due to concerns over Romania's ability to deliver on a number of key commitments. Only agreement on unique safeguard mechanisms allowed accession negotiations to be concluded on 14 December. The Treaty of

---

[13] *Joint Declaration: One Europe*, Official Journal of the European Union, L236, 23 September 2003, p. 971.

Accession was then finalised and signed in Luxembourg on 25 April 2005.[14] In the meantime the Commission issued a positive opinion on 22 February 2005,[15] and the EP gave its formal assent to Romania's accession on 13 April 2005.

Since its signature, the Treaty of Accession has been with the EU member states and the acceding states for ratification, a process expected to last around eighteen months. The process began well with the Romanian parliament unanimously (434 v 0 votes) approving the Treaty on 17 May 2005, and by the end of the 2005, Cyprus, Czech Republic, Estonia, Greece, Hungary, Italy, Slovakia, Slovenia and Spain had all completed ratification. Latvia, Malta, the Netherlands and the United Kingdom followed suit in early 2006.

Assuming the remaining 12 member states have completed ratification in time, Romania should accede to the EU on 1 January 2007. This is what the Treaty of Accession envisages. However, the treaty contains a number of safeguard clauses. A first allows the EU member states, acting by a qualified majority, to delay accession by one year if Romania fails to fulfil specified commitments concerning competition policy, a Schengen Action Plan, external borders, reform of the judiciary, anti-corruption measures, police reform, an anti-crime strategy, state aids, and a steel restructuring programme. In addition there is a general one year delay mechanism applicable to Bulgaria and Romania that the EU's member states can trigger by unanimity if 'there is a serious risk of either of those States being manifestly unprepared to meet the requirements of membership'.[16] No such clauses were necessary in the context of the 2004 enlargement, nor are their other precedents.

Whether the safeguard mechanisms will be used remains to be seen. Any decision will be made on the basis of a Commission monitoring report to be published in October 2006. Already, however, warning letters have been sent to Bucharest detailing areas in which further reform and action is needed if the 2007 target for accession is to be met. Furthermore an initial Commission monitoring report published in October 2005 indicated that there were 'a number of areas of serious concern' that required 'immediate and decisive action'. This included aspects of the justice and home affairs *acquis*, the fight against fraud and corruption, and administrative capacity for implementing

---

[14] *Treaty between... the member states of the European Union and the Republic of Bulgaria and Romania concerning the accession of the Republic of Bulgaria and Romania to the European Union*, Official Journal of the European Union, L157, 21 June 2005.

[15] European Commission, *Opinion on the applications for accession to the European Union by the Republic of Bulgaria and Romania*, COM(2005)55 final, Brussels, 22 February 2005.

[16] *Protocol concerning the conditions and arrangements for admission of Bulgaria and Romania to the European Union*, Official Journal of the European Union, L157, 21 June 2005, Article 39.

the environmental *acquis*.[17] Progress was made in addressing these in the following months. Consequently, and although concerns about the state of judicial reform and border security in particular were still being voiced, a consensus appeared to be emerging in early 2006 that enough was being done to enable accession to take place on 1 January 2007.[18]

CONCLUSION

Accession to the EU will be an immensely significant political step for Romania. It will not only signal acceptance into a community of states committed to shared values and ideas, but it will also bring greater certainty with regard to the country's future economic and political orientation. This is not to say that membership will be without its challenges. Given past and indeed persistent concerns about Romania's capacity to meet its obligations in preparing for accession to the EU, the country can expect to be closely monitored for compliance with the requirements of membership once it joins. Membership will not be an easy ride.

It will nevertheless have been achieved, and the importance of this for the future of Romania should no be overlooked. As with membership of the Council of Europe and of NATO, membership of the EU is clearly viewed as confirming the country's 'Europeanness'. Romania will be seen as an integral part of 'Europe' and will have opportunities to play a fuller role in determining the future of European integration. Membership of all the main organizations of Euro-Atlantic integration also confirms the break with the country's communist past. It confirms too that the transition from dictatorship to democracy has been completed and that Romania is now a functioning market economy.

The road to full participation in the structures of Euro-Atlantic integration has not, however, been one that Romania has either easily or quickly negotiated. It has been a demanding process necessitating considerable and often painful domestic reforms in Romania. It is also a process that has lasted more than a decade and a half. And were it not for the dynamics of NATO and EU enlargement it could have taken longer. Romania has clearly at times struggled to come to terms with what integration either requires or involves. It has also struggled to convince the various organizations both that it meets the criteria for accession and that its membership is in the interest of all concerned. Those struggles appear now to be in the past.

[17] European Commission, *Romania: 2005 Comprehensive Monitoring Report*, COM(2005) 534 final, Brussels, 25 October 2005.

[18] See 'Bulgaria and Romania told to speed up reforms', *Financial Times*, 22 February 2006 (via www.ft.com).

The Road to the European Union

CHAPTER FIVE

How Fit is Romania's Economy to Join the EU?

Daniel Daianu

Romania's gross domestic product (GDP) grew by an annual average of above 5% during 2000–2004 and a similar rate was expected in 2005. Inflation came down to 9.3% in 2003 (from over 40% in 2000) and a further drop, to around 8% was likely in 2005; inflation is forecast to diminish to below 6% in 2006. Fiscal consolidation has been under way for several years now. The private sector produces almost 70% of GDP while the banking sector is on a sound foot. These results have helped the dialogue with the European Commission and allowed Romania to sign a Treaty of Accession to the European Union (EU) on 25 April 2005. Romania's scheduled accession in 2007 and catching up prospects hinge on continuing with structural reforms.

Countries aspiring to join the EU are asked to comply with two fundamental requirements: to have a 'functioning market economy'; and to be able to withstand competitive pressures in the internal market and, eventually, economic and monetary union. The first requirement – the existence of a functioning market economy[1] – connotes an institutional set up (the functioning of basic market institutions) which would enable, *inter alia*, effective financial discipline, proper law enforcement and the protection of property rights, effective financial intermediation, and an adequate policy mix framework ensuring efficacy in dealing with powerful adverse shocks. The

---

[1] A 'functioning market economy' is quite curious terminologically. The notion cannot be found in economic textbooks, since all market economies are functioning, whether well or bad. What the experts in Brussels have, most likely, in mind is a 'well functioning market economy' which relies on a sound institutional setup and low information and transaction costs for the sake of necessary resource reallocation.

second demand takes cognisance of the dramatic reduction of the scope of national economic policy in a region where *inter alia* intra-trade barriers no longer exist, capital flows freely, a single currency and one monetary policy operate in 12 (out of the 15) old member states, and, in a softer form, the Exchange Rate Mechanism (ERM2) significantly constrains exchange rate policy in the new member states. Both exigencies are seen as essential for enhancing nominal and real convergence, without which the EU would be undermined from within.

As a matter fact, the lack of sufficient convergence inside the EU and competitive pressures from outside, as well as increasingly strained welfare systems, point to a more complicated picture when it comes to explaining the sources of economic performance and fitness for membership. The Lisbon Agenda is a reflection of this reality check, but also of the inability of many EU member states to find adequate responses to global competition and social strain. The results of the 2005 referenda in France and the Netherlands, and the economic woes of Italy in particular as well as of other EU member states are telling in this respect. It is against this backdrop that one can judge the growing suspicion vis-à-vis further enlargement to low-wage countries among citizens of 'Old Europe' and the more severe scrutiny Romania is facing in its quest to join the EU in 2007. Fears of outsourcing and off-shoring have influenced political discourse more and more in some wealthy economies in recent years.

There is a further angle from which Romania's quest to join the EU can be judged: the capacity to cope with the challenge of development over the long term. With a *per capita* income of 30% of the EU average Romania has a long way to go in this regard. Continuing with structural reforms will enhance the ability of the country to catch up economically.

WHERE DOES ROMANIA'S ECONOMY COME FROM?

At the end of the 1980s Romania was one of the few remaining archetypical command systems left in Europe. Her economy was exhausted after a policy of repaying the entire external debt ahead of schedule whereas the living standards of the population had plummeted. The 1990s present a complicated story of transition in Romania.[2] Major disputes concerning privatization, the pace of economic reforms, and attitudes towards foreign capital translated into political fighting that influenced the coherence and consistency of reform policy. The issue of the renewal of bureaucratic and political elites and ensuing

---

[2]   Daianu, D. *Transformation as a Real Process* (Aldershot: Ashgate, 1998).

tensions should be highlighted in this context. Romania experienced an economic evolution full of twists and turns, of the boom and bust type, with major fluctuations of output and persistent high inflation.

The Boom and Bust Cycle: 1990–1999

Romania witnessed its first transitional recession (as other transition countries did) and three digit inflation rates during 1990–1992. A positive dynamic of overall output and diminishing inflation occurred during 1993–1996, while the private sector was steadily, albeit slowly, gaining ground in the economy. Big privatization deals were still waiting to occur and soft budget constraints were ubiquitous. The state owned banks were the main vehicles for providing subsidies to loss-making companies. Because of insufficient restructuring, strains kept accumulating in the economy during this period and these strains showed up in the rapid increase of foreign debt and in difficulties in financing external deficits. Heavy borrowing on international capital markets could not prevent the official foreign exchange reserves of the country from falling below US$ 700 million at the end of 1996 by when monthly inflation had returned to double digits. The period of growth was grinding to a halt and the need for a severe adjustment was looming.

Policy change and adjustment in 1997 relied on further price liberalization, the unification of the exchange rate, massive cuts in subsidies, and a speeding-up of privatization. The policy turnaround invigorated the stock exchange for a while and replenished the reserves of the National Bank of Romania (NBR). With the benefit of hindsight, that policy change arguably protected Romania from the worst consequences of the contagion which engulfed world financial markets after the fall of the Thai bath in late 1997. But an economic downturn was unavoidable owing to the toughness of austerity measures and policy inconsistencies. GDP declined by 15% during 1997–1999. Arguably, economic policy at the time underestimated the structural rigidities embedded in the Romanian economy and the need to deal with monopolies and foster competition.

1999 brought another shock: peak debt service payments of US$ 2.8 billion were due in that year and at a time of extreme nervousness on world financial markets. This situation raised the spectre of external default, which was reinforced by the International Monetary Fund's new philosophy of burden sharing with private investors. Practically denied access to international private capital markets due to exorbitant spreads, Romania could avert default only by an exceptional balance of payments adjustment involving substantial expenditure switching and cutting that almost halved the current account deficit.

Economic Recovery/Growth Since 2000

2000 revealed signs of economic recovery: the fall of economic activity was reversed, inflation started again to come down and an export boom took place. GDP rose by 2.1% and inflation came down to 40.7%. Significantly, too, although Romania experienced troubles on its financial markets during 2000, the banking system withstood the pressure and continued its convalescence following the failure of two major state owned banks. At the same time, the private sector's share in the banking system increased considerably. Growth speeded up during 2001–2003, when it hovered around 5% (see Table 5.1). In 2004 it jumped to over 8% owing to a remarkable harvest. For 2005 the growth rate was set to stay around 5%. During all this period fiscal consolidation has been under way. In 2004 the budget deficit came down to -1.1%. For 2005 the budget deficit will probably stay below -1.0% of GDP in spite of the effects of the year's widespread flooding. The progress with disinflation is particularly commendable for Romania was an outlier in this regard until recently. These results prompted upgrades from the main rating agencies. Thus, Romania got an improved investment grade from Fitch in 2004 of BBB- and a similar grade from Standard and Poor the following year.

A major novelty of 2005 was fiscal policy reform via a 16% flat tax aimed at boosting inward foreign direct investment (FDI) and making the economy more transparent.[3] A downside of this policy move has been its pro-cyclical nature, at a time of a rapidly growing internal demand and external deficits. What has spoiled the picture somewhat lately is the surge in the current account deficit, which grew to 6.9% of GDP in 2004 (compared to 5.6% in 2003 and 3.6% in 2002). By including non-repatriated profits this deficit came close to 7.8%. For 2005 the current account deficit is likely to exceed 9% of GDP owing to the expansion of domestic credit and exchange rate appreciation. The surge in imports includes machinery and equipment, which is good for industrial renewal. However, the speed of the rise in external deficits is to be watched carefully. Recent measures by the NBR aimed at diminishing the growth of hard currency denominated non-governmental credit should be seen from this perspective. The volume of FDI, which stood at over €12 billion at the end of 2004, is much below the volume registered in Poland, Hungary and the Czech Republic. Inward FDI is needed in order to restructure and modernize the real economy, energy production and distribution included.

[3]   For an assessment of the informal economy in Romania see Albu, L. et al, *The Underground Economy in Romania* (Bucharest: CEROPE, 2001), mimeo.

Table 5.1: Evolution of Main Macroeconomic Indicators in Romania

	2000	2001	2002	2003	2004	2005*
Real GDP, % change	2.1	5.7	4.9	4.8	8.3	5.0
Inflation (CPI) (end December)	40.7	30.3	17.8	14.1	9.3	8.0
Unemployment	10.5	8.8	8.4	7.4	6.2	5.8
Budget Deficit	-3.5	-3.3	-2.7	-2.3	-1.1	-0.8
Current Account Deficit	-5.7	-5.6	-3.6	-5.8	-6.9	-9.0
External Debt						
% GDP	30	31	35	32	30	31
% exports	80	81	85	85	81	80

Source: National statistics and own estimates; * own forecasts

Economic Performance: Pluses and Minuses

Romania's economic performance has improved substantially in recent years and it may be instructive to compare this with the situation of some new EU member states one year before they joined the EU (see Table 5.2).[4] The improvements are significant since they motivated the European Commission to grant Romania the status of a 'functioning market economy' in 2004. But this status cannot obscure significant weaknesses with regard to financial discipline, the enforcement of market regulations, the transparency and stability of the regulatory framework, the public administration and the judiciary, and the strain in the pensions system. The deepening of reforms is needed to make the economy stronger and capable of withstanding pressures inside the EU.

ECONOMIC PROGRESS TO BUILD UPON

Romania's economic advance should be judged from two perspectives: one that looks at structural changes in the economy, and one focused on macroeconomic policy. On the first, the steady expansion of the private sector in the economy has been accompanied by more entrepreneurial drive, more capital formation and export orientation. The private sector's contribution to GDP formation is

[4] For an insightful comparison between the new EU Member States, on the one hand, and Bulgaria and Romania, on the other, see Koromzay, V. (2005), 'Comments' in Detken, C. et al (eds), *The New EU Member States. Convergence and Stability – Third ECB Central Banking Conference, 21–22 October 2004* (Frankfurt am Main: European Central Bank, 2005), pp. 63–67. See also Lanzeni, L.M., 'Romania on the way towards the EU: A convergence assessment', presentation made at the *European Financial Forum*, Bucharest, 22 June 2005.

Table 5.2: Key Macroeconomic Indicators Compared to Maastricht Criteria: EU Candidate Countries One Year Before They Got into the Union (2003) and Romania in 2004

	Budget deficit (% of GDP)	Public debt (% of GDP)	Inflation (%)	Interest rate on 10 years € bond (%)	Exchange rate stability
Target	‹-3	60	<2.8	<6.8	Yes
Czech Republic	-7.8	34.5	0.4	4.63 (23.6.2014)	No
Hungary	-5.5	56.8	4.7	5.5 (6.5.2014)	No
Poland	-4.6	44.8	0.8	4.5 (5.2.2013)	No
Slovakia	-5.2	43.8	8.1	4.5 (20.5.2014)	No
Romania	-1.1	27.0	9.3	-	No

Source: Countries' national banks

nearing 70% while it accounts for over 55% of social capital in the economy and more than 70% of the employed population. There has also been a significant rise in foreign trade and integration into EU markets. Trade with the EU represents 70% of overall trade. The openness of the economy is also indicated by the share of foreign capital in the banking industry and telecommunications; energy markets are also opening rapidly, even more so than in some of the old EU member countries.

The banking system is much sounder nowadays after a massive clean up operation in the late 1990s and the introduction of a new regulatory framework that fits the Bank of International Settlements' new recommendations. This evolution has taken place against a background of increasing foreign ownership in the banking sector (to above 60% of total assets and loans at the end of 2004),[5] which has ameliorated corporate governance. The banking system has increased its capacity to provide effective intermediation between savers and investors, and lending and borrowing rates have decreased substantially. The range of financial products has increased remarkably and has fuelled non-governmental credit;[6] the latter has boomed by 70%, in real terms, in the last couple of years. It is noticeable that despite this rise prudential indicators are still in safe territory.[7] The non-banking financial sector has developed rapidly;

[5] The privatization of Banca Comerciala Romana and the Romanian Savings Bank (CEC) would raise this share.
[6] The annual yield for t-bills, which was a major attraction for banks' investment policy, decreased from 76.0% in 1999 and 35.7% in 2001 to 17.3% in 2002 and 8% in June 2005. This has prompted banks to orient increasingly toward consumer and production finance.
[7] Even if some numbers are likely to be overstated, the overall picture evinces a remarkable turnaround compared to the late 1990s.

Table 5.3: Key Prudential Indicators in the Banking System

	1999	2000	2001	2002	2003	2004
Solvency rate (>12%)	17.9	23.7	28.8	25.0	21.09	18.79
Bad loans, as % of total assets	2.36	0.29	0.32	0.23	0.22	0.18
Credit risk rate	35.4	3.8	2.5	1.1	3.37	2.85

Source: NBR statistics (monthly bulletins). Capital adequacy - net assets / total assets; Credit risk - unadjusted exposure relative to loans and interest under 'doubtful' or 'loss'/ total loans and interest excluding off-balance sheet items

the best indicator is the market capitalization of the Bucharest Stock Exchange: from 1.04% of GDP in 1999 and 3.3% of GDP in 2001, it moved to 8% of GDP in 2003 and 14% of GDP in the first half of 2005.

An adequate macroeconomic policy mix has under-lied disinflation (see Table 5.1 above). The NBR has focused more clearly on fighting inflation and has been helped by fiscal consolidation. Although significant quasi-fiscal deficits blur this positive assessment, it is encouraging that they have shown a tendency to decline lately. Likewise, budget subsidies have declined steadily and energy prices have come close to EU wide levels. This improves resource allocation and cost management, though it is quite painful for people on low incomes.

The openness of the economy has also been broadened functionally by capital account liberalization, which is almost complete (access of non-residents to local bank accounts was allowed in April 2005). Capital account liberalization has been quite complicated because of relatively high interest rate differentials and substantial speculative inflows. The NBR has been walking on a tight rope in this respect, but it has done it commendably. A negative fallout could result, however, from a further big surge in external deficits owing to the appreciation of the Romanian currency and the big rise of domestic credit. It should be said that capital account liberalization is a prerequisite for EU accession,[8] and relates to direct inflation targeting as a new monetary policy regime. Inflation targeting was adopted by the NBR officially in August 2005 reflecting the NBR's wish to bolster its operational independence and focus more effectively on reducing inflation.

---

[8] Capital account liberalization in Romania can be seen as optimization under severe constraints, for interest rate differentials and low monetization (share of financial intermediation in GDP) would have justified a more gradual process. EU accession, however, demands full capital account liberalization at the time of entry.

What Clouds The Sky?

Serious weaknesses nevertheless persist in the Romanian economy and these could harm macroeconomic conditions and GDP growth over the longer term unless they are addressed consistently. This caveat does not refer to unavoidable business cycle related fluctuations, but to a possible relapse into revived inflation and balance of payments difficulties. These weaknesses are rooted in:

- Loss-making companies that produce sizeable arrears and quasi-fiscal deficits. Current disinflation puts pressure on these companies and unless restructuring makes more headway persistent large quasi-fiscal deficits will hit the public budget in years to come.
- Budget revenues are below 30% of GDP while financing needs are bulging. Unless tax collection improves considerably Romania faces a budget 'shock' at the moment of accession because of inescapable financial obligations (e.g. co-financing of EU funds; EU budget contribution). Consequently, the budget deficit could rise again above 3% of GDP, which would worsen public finances. It would also involve a further rise in the current account deficit which might be unsustainable and eventually cause a sharp depreciation of the Leu and consequently an increase in inflation.
- The investment climate is plagued by administrative and red tape barriers, and by corruption.
- A pensions system under increasing strain. The pensions system is in fact unbalanced, with much of its financing coming from the health insurance budget. The problem is of a chronic nature because the number of the retired population exceeds the official number of employees (the ratio is nowadays 3:2 as compared to 1:2 in the early 1990s). An unreformed pensions system will strain the public budget in years to come.
- A burdensome agricultural sector. This is an issue of concern in Romania's relations with the EU. About 35–38% of the population lives in rural areas, while agriculture contributes a mere 12% to Romania's GDP and hardly, if at all, to the public budget. The future of Romanian farmers is not at present a topic of much public debate, and the level of awareness of what EU accession involves is quite low. In the EU there is an increasing propensity to reform the Common Agricultural Policy (CAP) further for the sake of reducing agricultural subsidies and to allocate more funds to advanced R&D-related activities. Romania would be adversely affected by such a reordering of priorities.
- Rigid labour markets. Unemployment has been kept at a reasonable level because many Romanians have found an outlet abroad. Some estimates put the number of Romanian citizens who work abroad well over one million. Hopefully, changes in the labour code under way will redress this situation.

Policy Dilemmas and Challenges

The weaknesses mentioned above and developmental challenges create major policy dilemmas which Romanian policy-makers need to address carefully in the run-up to EU accession. The effectiveness of the policy mix needs to be secured amid a series of at least five trade-offs:

- Tight budget deficits that should help bring inflation down to 4% by 2007, while necessary infrastructure projects demand substantial public financing.
- Minimal trade protection and substantial exchange rate appreciation could entail further rises in the current account deficit so that the burden of adjustment would increasingly fall on the public budget; the overburdening of the budget would be deepened by inflation targeting.
- Strong exchange rate appreciation because of substantial capital inflows (including growing remittances from Romanians who work abroad – €2.5 billion in 2004). This could cause a 'Dutch disease'[9] unless productivity gains are adequate. The Italian syndrome should be a lesson in this respect!
- Interest rates cuts, while capital account liberalisation proceeds further, may widen external deficits.
- The current type of competitiveness (based on wage differentials) versus the innovation-driven type of economies, with which Romania is trying to converge (Romania's spending on research and development is seven times lower than the Lisbon target of 3% of GDP).[10]

The dilemmas sketched above constrain policy heavily. They suggest at the same time policy guidelines. In terms of economic and market structure there is need to harden budget constraints in the energy sector and to streamline state aid – which should in any case fit EU requirements. Indeed, failing to meet obligations regarding state aid could trigger a safeguard clause in the Treaty of Accession and delay Romania's membership of the EU. Privatization in the energy sector can bring in massive, badly needed inward foreign investment and help modernization and restructuring decisively. But energy markets, like financial markets, have to be well regulated so that market abuse can be prevented, something that is particularly important in a much less affluent society. Experiences worldwide should be a lesson to Romanian policy-makers.

---

[9] 'Dutch disease' refers to a financial bonanza that befalls a country following the discovery of, for example, major oil fields. Greatly increased oil-related export revenues would appreciate the national currency considerably and harm the manufacturing sector unless, ultimately, adequate productivity gains are achieved.

[10] However, it has to be acknowledged that the crux of the matter for the Romanian economy – as an emerging economy – lies more in absorbing than in inventing new technologies.

Tax collection and the broadening of the tax base have to improve considerably so that the co-financing of EU funded policies and the provision of public goods respond to Romanian economy's needs without entailing unsustainable budget deficits. It would be great to see budget revenues go up by at least, 4–5% of GDP in a few years' time. Multiannual budget programming will help set policy priorities according to judicious, long-term cost-benefit analysis. The ongoing crisis of the pensions system puts an additional burden on the public budget; a new pensions system is needed.

A rapid expansion of rural credit mechanisms (which could involve the efficient use of EU rural development funds) and land consolidation would be among the solutions for rural development. The fate of Romanian agriculture depends on how the CAP will be shaped in the years to come and on how Romania will use the EU financial assistance oriented toward this sector.

Another big challenge is to increase the capacity to absorb EU funds. EU financial assistance (structural and cohesion funds) could supplement budget revenues substantially and increase the provision of essential public goods (infrastructure, education and health care). EU assistance would also bring in other funding, from private and public sources. But the track record of absorption is poor and unless this capacity grows significantly EU funds may diminish in the future. They may also diminish given the dispute between net contributors and net beneficiaries over the structure of the EU budget. Spain's experience in using EU funds should be studied by Romanian policy-makers. An idea to consider is to form a financial institution with the aim of using public and private funds in order to help develop infrastructure. Privatization revenues and long-term bond issues by this institution, plus other mobilized resources, could be channelled toward financing badly needed projects. The latter would have to be prioritised in view of the modernization challenges facing the Romanian economy and Romania's obligations towards the EU as well as the need to relieve the public budget of excessive strain.

Romania needs to spend substantially more on education and R&D as a strategy for its long-term economic development, even if local research and development would be linked primarily to the assimilation of imported technology. This is quite normal in an emerging economy that tries to capitalize on the world stock of knowledge. A challenge is to reduce the dependency on labour-intensive production, which is increasingly dominated by low wage Asian manufacturers. The expected and unavoidable rise in wages in the years to come could price out many firms in labour intensive production unless productivity gains are commensurate and higher value added products are gaining in output share.

The Romanian economy has distinct characteristics that demand careful consideration of appropriate monetary and exchange rate policies. Low monetisation and the wide use of the euro and the US dollar in local transactions complicate the conduct of monetary policy.[11] Likewise, the large stock of arrears and potential future pressures on the government budget – such as the high cost of pensions expenditure or fiscal costs in the run up to EU entry – require enhanced co-ordination of monetary and exchange rate policies with budgetary policy. The NBR has, as noted, recently introduced inflation targeting. Arguably, a 'soft' form of inflation targeting through a gradual introduction is appropriate.[12] This soft monetary framework would focus on inflation but would consider shorter horizons (two-four quarters) rather than the medium term.[13] It would not neglect the exchange rate completely and would work closely with the government on budget policy. Full capital account liberalization would coincide with EU accession.

The labour code needs attention too. It has to protect workers against abuses. But it also has to make labour markets flexible enough so that industrial and economic restructuring occurs at an appropriate speed. Romania should not get into the sort of mess one encounters in some of the old EU member countries. The labour code issue brings to the fore the question of the model towards which the Romanian economy should evolve.

WHICH EUROPEAN MODEL?

Arguably, the European model places an emphasis on the need to preserve social cohesion and extols the virtues of social solidarity. On the other hand, the welfare state, although in varied forms, is a ubiquitous trait of advanced capitalism worldwide. And some convergence between models has taken place in the last couple of decades under the spell of globalization. Likewise, inside Europe, too, there is significant social and economic variety, which makes people differentiate between a Scandinavian model (with its emphasis on social redistribution, but quite flexible labour markets), a 'core' model in Germany and France, the British model (which is closer to the American model), and a Mediterranean model, which seems to be of a more 'disorderly' sort (although the bulging budget deficits in Germany and France have cast some doubt on this view lately). Likewise, some newer EU member states from Central and Eastern Europe practice a more liberal (in the European sense) form of market economy.

---

[11] See also Antohi, D. et al, 'The Transmission Mechanism of Monetary Policy in Romania', *National Bank of Romania Working Paper*, no.13, 2003; Citu, F., *Monetary Policy. The Romanian Way*, Bucharest, 11 May 2005, manuscript.

[12] Daianu, D. and Kallai, E., *Disinflation and Monetary Policy Arrangements in Romania*, WDI Working Paper, 789, November 2004 (www.wdi.umich.edu/files/Publications/Working Papers/wp789.pdf).

[13] This is because the required transformation of the Romanian economy that is still needed complicates the tasks of econometric modelling, which is a must for direct inflation targeting.

The EU project does influence national public policies by spreading common standards and imposing common rules for policy-makers and institutions. However, it is constrained by a highly visible contradiction between its entrenched welfare model and the need to make markets more flexible. This contradiction would not be so acutely felt in the absence of the tremendous pressures exerted by globalization, by competition from low wage economies including from Eastern Europe. Globalization, in particular the economic rise of Asia, undermines the lavish welfare state in Western Europe. Social assistance and pension systems are being overhauled. This is a painful and politically very sensitive undertaking and is taking place against the background of population ageing. The experiences of Finland, Denmark and Sweden in going from welfare to *workfare* provide interesting policy venues for other EU member countries.

Although globalization has a non-trivial ideological component the forces at work have acquired a powerful momentum of their own, which is driven by technological change and intensified competition. The latter can be restrained by bouts of protectionism (in trade and competitive devaluations) and security concerns, but its power seems to be unstoppable. The rise of China and India in the world economy changes hierarchies and can turn non-zero into zero-sum economic games. From this come fears of outsourcing and off-shoring.[14] For it is quite impossible to compete with economies where labour costs are 10, 15, or even 20 times lower, other conditions being fairly similar.

Romania has to adopt EU rules. But it needs to do so in such a way that allows its economy to improve its performance steadily and for catching up to become a reality. Romania's labour costs are considerably lower than in most EU member countries, but similarly lower is its overall productivity. Therefore, which 'European model' to evolve towards is a relevant policy issue for Romanian policy-makers and business leaders.

FINAL REMARKS: THE EU'S ROLE

In spite of the results of the 2005 referenda in France and the Netherlands, the EU is a stark, indisputable reality and it will stay as such for the foreseeable future. For most European non-EU member countries the big political and economic 'game' is to join the *Union*.

The EU can play an exceptional part in Romania's transformation and modernization drive and is faced with an extraordinary opportunity to overcome the trap of backwardness, to accomplish a secular quest for modernization. It

---

[14] For a very insightful paper on why globalization (free trade) may cause a lot of friction see Samuelson, P. 'Where Ricardo and Mill Rebut and Confirm Arguments of Mainstream Economists Supporting Globalization', *Journal of Economic Perspectives*, 18 (3) 2004, 135–47.

should be noted that Romania has an income *per capita* that represents roughly 30% of the EU average and at the same time is a country with a relatively large population (22 million). Under the hypothesis of an average rate of economic growth of 5% over the longer run with the EU average rate of economic growth being 2%, and considering the Balassa-Samuelson effect, Romania would need 10–12 years to reach half the average *per capita* income in the EU. The catching-up of the average *per capita* income (at purchasing power parity) would take about two generations assuming that a substantial growth differential in Romania's favour is maintained.

Sustained economic progress would require higher saving and investment ratios in Romania, a public policy geared to the development of human capital and infrastructure, and Romanians increasingly using what new information and communication technologies offer.[15] Romania would have to absorb EU structural and cohesion funds fully. But such evolutions depend, in turn, on the functioning of institutions: a strengthening of the judiciary and the rule of law; competent, honest and innovative central and local public administrations; a solid financial and banking system; good structures of corporate governance orientated towards higher economic performances; an education system offering equal chances to children and adults; laws that enjoy social acceptance; and a favourable social ethos. The quality of public policy itself depends on the functioning of institutions.[16]

It is pure naiveté to believe that openness towards a wider economic space where asymmetries, agglomeration effects and cumulative causality are present would ensure, *ipso facto*, economic development. In today's world extraordinary opportunities can coexist with failures of large proportions. If one accepts that not any kind of integration brings about benefits,[17] it makes sense to judge EU accession as a possible solution to the secular desire of economic development and modernization of the country. This could provide the institutional and technological 'Big Push' Romania needs in order to reduce the economic gaps that separate it from more developed European countries.[18] But it does matter how Romania accedes to the EU and how it will fare afterwards. The key here is to make the benefits of accession outweigh its costs.

[15] See 'Romania and The Lisbon Agenda', *GEA-CEROPE Report*, Bucharest, 2004, p. 30.

[16] For why good institutions are essential for long-term growth see Helpman, E. *The Mystery of Economic Growth* (Cambridge MA: Harvard University Press, 2004).

[17] Rodrik, D. *The New Global Economy and Developing Countries. Making Openness Work* (Washington DC: Overseas Development Council. 2000).

[18] Writing more than five decades ago, Rosenstein-Rodan talked about the need of a 'Big Push' for Southeastern Europe, in order for it to catch up economically with the West. See Rosenstein-Rodan, P., 'Problems of Industrialization of Eastern and South eastern Europe', *Economic Journal*, 53 (1943), 202–211.

CHAPTER SIX

Civil Society and the Media in Romania

Baroness Nicholson of Winterbourne

In communist-era Romania, civil society and an independent media were recognised by the authorities as potential sources of challenge to the regime. They were therefore systematically stifled. Fifteen years since the demise of Ceaușescu, the condition of Romanian civil society and of her media is now an indicator of the state of health of Romanian democracy.

The development of these two aspects of Romanian national life has not, however, been equally positive. The Romanian media remains a subject of continual controversy, but it has recently emerged from a long and dark period when its independence and integrity were under threat, and can now be said to be both free and dynamic. By contrast, civil society (with some honourable exceptions) remains generally weak and etiolated, partly due to overdependence on donor funds.

My own in-depth experience of these issues has largely come about through my work as *rapporteur* for Romania in the European Parliament (EP). EP reports on Romania's progress towards European Union (EU) membership have consistently focused on human rights and fundamental freedoms, with particular emphasis on freedom of media. My perspective is also very much informed by the issue of child protection, with which I have been closely involved for many years. The problem of child protection provides a telling illustration of the relationship between Romanian civil society and the media, and this chapter examines the issue closely.

Observing the Romanian media scene is as fascinating as was observing the media scene in London during the 1980s when Rupert Murdoch brought radical change to the way that newspapers were managed in the United Kingdom. Although Romania has not experienced such a violent and dramatic series of confrontations, the management and ownership changes that have taken place in Bucharest in recent years are equally dramatic in their own way, and observing how the media interacts with Romanian political life is particularly instructive.

A quick overview of the Romanian media scene would have to include *Jurnalul Naţional, Adevârul, Evenimentul Zilei, Cotidiânul* as well as the satirical weekly paper *Academia Caţavencu*. Regarding the TV stations *TVR* (Romanian Television) and *Realitatea* (Reality) must be mentioned as well as the state-run *Radio România Actualităţi* (Radio Romania News). In essence, it must be said that the Romanian media is overall in rude health and the publications mentioned here are profitable. The business is fiercely competitive and journalistic standards are being continually driven up. Although the Social Democrat (PSD) government of 2000–2004 tried to seize some control of the Romanian media agenda – leading to protests from Romania's civil society and warnings from the EU – it has bounced back under the new government. However, there is a glut of unprofitable smaller newspapers which are sustained by factors other than profit, such as the local politician-cum-businessman who requires a media mouthpiece and is willing to subsidise it. There are also a growing number of English language publications available to the large number of ex-pats who either live in or visit Bucharest (see below).

On the quality side of the Romanian newspaper scene *Jurnalul Naţional* stands out. *Jurnalul Naţional* is Romania's biggest quality publication with a readership of almost half a million people, and is part of a growing media empire, including the leading private TV station *Antena 1*. Many Romanian intellectuals are, however, deeply suspicious of *Jurnalul Naţional* because of the somewhat ambiguous status of its owner, who leads Romania's conservative party. *Jurnalul Naţional* is an interesting publication from a number of perspectives. Every Monday it publishes a 'collectors' edition' with an in-depth analysis of Romania's troubled history under Communism making the newspaper a self-appointed 'history teacher to the nation'. Its journalistic and investigative standards are high, and its use of photos is superb, but like many newspapers it draws the line at investigating its own owners when their integrity is called into question, and is unable to resist the temptation of presenting the views of its proprietor under the guise of independent journalism. *Jurnalul Naţional* also has a much bigger marketing budget than other Romanian papers and was offering readers a brand new *Dacia Logan* every day in May 2005, resulting in a surge in sales during that month – and these figures have been heavily promoted ever since to show that it is the market leader.

Evenimentul Zilei and *Adevârul* are also high quality publications which have both survived tremendous management upheavals in the last year. The drama at *Evenimentul Zilei* (Daily Events) took place in 2004 and started when the Swiss media group Ringier took over the newspaper and wanted to get rid of the outspoken editor (and founder) of the newspaper, Cornel Nistorescu. His dismissal led to the resignation of over 50 of the journalistic staff, many of whom ended up on the *Cotidiânul (The Daily)* newspaper which has emerged as one of the best papers on the Romanian market. A similar revolution took place at the venerable *Adevârul* (The Truth), a newspaper that was once seen as one of the best on the Romanian market but has fallen low in recent years. The storm at *Adevârul* was caused by the resignation of journalistic icon Cristian Tudor Popescu, whose departure was followed by the resignation of the editorial board as well as over 50 of the editorial staff, all of whom proceeded to set up a brand new daily newspaper called *Gândul* (The Thought), a quality publication that quickly established itself and began to turn a profit within a month.

There are various observations that we can draw from these editorial upheavals. Many people were surprised that *Evenimentul Zilei* and *Adevârul* survived as newspapers after the loss of their iconic editors – both of whom appear regularly on TV and radio chat shows with instant commentary on everything from terrorism to football – and it is clear that most Romanians associate these newspapers with these charismatic editors. But both papers did survive and *Evenimentul Zilei* in particular seems to be doing very well. This says something about the residual strength of the Romanian media market, the value of these brands, and that most readers are ultimately loyal to the newspaper rather than the editors.

The final newspaper to mention is the weekly satirical publication *Academia Cațavencu* (a name that is apparently without English translation). What is of particular interest about *Academia Cațavencu* is not so much its mockery of all those in power (in the style of Britain's *Private Eye*, making devastating use of photos of politicians and speech bubbles) but its ownership structure. On the one hand, *Academia Cațavencu* is seen by students, intellectuals and liberal-minded politicians as the one place where the hubris of those in power is challenged and in-depth investigations are carried out into a range of difficult issues. On the other hand, however, the main shareholder of *Academia Cațavencu* is Sorin Ovidiu Vântu, a former fund manager who stands charged of bankrupting a bank and robbing the nation's savings fund, which led to the penury of thousands of Romanian families. Under the former PSD government, Vântu was said to have immunity from arrest; regardless of the accuracy of this, it is no longer the case as he was recently given a suspended jail sentence for his financial misdemeanours. What is also interesting about the *Academia Cațavencu* group is that it has been very successful financially and has embarked on a media spending spree that has resulted in the purchase of a radio station, two women's magazines and the daily *Cotidiânul*.

Consolidation is the buzzword in the Romanian media these days and a few big groups – *Ringier* and the groups being formed around *Jurnalul Naţional* and *Academia Caţavencu* in particular – are gradually taking over the main publications. The smaller publications are being squeezed out and some of them are diversifying and becoming more sensational.

It is worth considering the English language press in this analysis. Although these publications are only really distributed in Bucharest, where most of the ex-pats are concentrated, they do form a part of the Romanian media market. The main group in this sector is the Romanian language business magazine *BIZ*, a publication that grew out of the main English language business weekly, *Bucharest Business Review*. This is a decent and straightforward (and seemingly profitable) newspaper which has a less respected – but virtually identical in design – rival which is called *Bucharest Business Week*. While these two publications battle it out for the high end of the ex-pat business market, there are a plethora of dubious 'entertainment' magazines which suggest the existence of a high demand for such publications, and a healthy advertising market. There are also two English language daily papers in Bucharest: *Nine O'Clock* and *Bucharest Daily News*. Both of these papers look fairly similar to each other in design and are similar in quality (i.e. not very impressive, but useful when in Romania).[1]

---

[1] Until this year I never had much contact with these publications, but this was shattered by a recent encounter with the newest of these publications: *Bucharest Daily News*. Eager to increase its share of Romania's small ex-pat media market, the publication decided to tackle a controversial issue – Romania's banning of international adoptions – and published a large and very one-sided article in February 2006 which promoted the pro-ICA (inter country adoption) point of view. The article also included a rather crude attack on my position on this issue, something which is quite common as I am seen as the *bête noir* of the pro-ICA lobby. I would have ignored this article, but they kept misquoting me and insisting interviews and statements. It is quite interesting to note what happened next as it is indication of how journalistic ethics are applied in Romania and how their understanding of consensus is sometimes rather perverse. *Bucharest Daily News* sent me a seemingly endless list of questions as well as the following statement: 'several members of the European Parliament contacted our newsroom in order to underline the fact that your anti-international adoption outlook is not shared by all the MEPs'. I was staggered by this statement as surely no journalist believes that a motion can pass any parliament unanimously. Surely everyone knows that such things are only possible in a dictatorship. Any legislation or policy is subject to a debate and a sometimes fierce difference of opinion. In the EP we have never had sustained unanimity on any issue and I don't suppose we ever will. This encounter with the 'ex-pat media' in Romania was instructive from various points of view, and what I find particularly noteworthy is the fact that this local 'ex-pat' newspaper is the only publication in Romania that has mounted a sustained media campaign on behalf of the pro-ICA lobby. The Romanian media, in general, have to be congratulated by the fact that they have treated this issue with a lot more balance and common sense than was shown by *Bucharest Daily News*.

The electronic media have not undergone such dramatic changes as has been experienced by the mainstream Romanian newspapers , but the question of who will run the state-run TV station, *TVR*, as well as the national radio station, *Radio România Actualități*, continues to be a contentious issue. The directors of both of these media channels were appointed by the PSD government and were accused of being their lackies. But replacing them has been a long and difficult process as the new government is keen not to be charged with compromising press freedom by installing its own appointees, and procedures have therefore been followed. What has emerged at TVR, however, is worthy of mention here as a new director – who has no apparent political affiliations – has been appointed. This is a first for Romania. It also has to be mentioned that the quality of TV productions in Romania is generally very high, and they have started to produce their own soap operas, police serials as well as game shows. The quality of news is also good and there are now three TV channels which are dedicated entirely to news (*Realitatea, Național 24 and Antena 3*).

But how free is the media in Romania? As mentioned above, civil society in Romania has been loudly protesting about the lack of journalistic independence, the problem of media owners controlling journalistic agendas and the lack of responsibility that editors take. The EP has picked up some of these issues and made the following statement at the end of 2004:

> 'as far as freedom of expression is concerned, the legal position for journalists has improved, but [the EP] is alarmed at the growing number of serious physical assaults on investigative journalists and calls for efforts to be made to shed light on these cases; [the EP] is concerned also at the fact that many organisations active in the media field remain in a precarious economic situation, enabling the authorities to exert pressure; considers that further efforts are needed to guarantee the independence of the media more effectively; therefore encourages further steps to guarantee the complete assertion of freedom of expression'.[2]

These issues are serious ones and need to be considered.

It is important to note that the above quotation dates from 2004, during the time of the PSD government, when press freedoms came under much greater pressure than has been apparent under the current government. The PSD government had a sophisticated and effective media relations policy which apparently involved the centralisation of all ministerial advertising budgets with advertising being placed in certain favoured publications in return for

---

[2] European Parliament *Committee on Foreign Affairs PE 349.831 Resolution on Romania's progress towards accession*, EP Document P6_TA(2004)0111, 16 December 2004, point 8.

editorial favours. Also, in cases when journalists were subject to physical intimidation, the process of resolving these cases was particularly protracted. The fact that there appear to have been no recent cases of journalist beatings can only be a good sign.

One of the worrying issues that was raised by civil society and the EP was 'the fact that many organisations active in the media field remain in a precarious economic situation, enabling the authorities to exert pressure'.[3] Indeed, in Romania, the number of newspapers, magazines and also English language publications is quite staggering and one struggles to understand how these are financially sustained. As mentioned above, some of these newspapers are sustained by politicians who are keen to have a mouthpiece where they can present their views, promote their allies and also denounce their enemies. Others papers are sustained by advertising, an association which is itself not immune from unethical practices. All this was possible with the development of a rather opaque form of capitalism in Romania, with its very flexible system of justice, in which local 'barons' built up regional fiefdoms based on their control of local councils and resources.

There are two forces which are gradually cleaning up this situation and leading to greater press freedom: the reform of the justice system and the growth of western-style media channels which are less easy to corrupt than the kind of local arrangements that have dogged Romania. Indeed, one can see this process already under the current Băsescu/Tăriceanu government. Even though its proposed package of judicial reform was blocked by the constitutional court in July 2005, leading to the temporary resignation of the government, it now seems determined to drive ahead with judicial reform. Similarly, some of the regional 'barons' are being challenged by local courts and their grip on the local media is being relaxed. At the same time, the strength of the main newspapers and TV stations mentioned above is continually increasing. The next few years will hopefully see the plethora of unsustainable publications currently on the Romanian market begin to disappear as the forces of justice and the marketplace increase the pressure on them.

In response to recent enquires in Bucharest about the health of the Romanian media, a Bucharest-based diplomat reported that 'the jury is still out'. This should be interpreted as a positive sign, and about as good as it gets regarding media freedoms. The media, after all, is not truly free in any part of the world; there are just too many forces preventing the journalist from telling the pure unadulterated truth. For example, if one speaks to people from the United Kingdom, Italy or the United States, they will often tell you that the editorial

[3] Ibid

policy of their main national media channels is more-or-less established by big business (United States), the government (Italy) or the proprietors (United Kingdom), thus restricting the freedom of movement for journalists. If we look at the BBC, for example, there is a long history of how successive British governments have tried to influence its news agenda, fortunately without much success. However, this is indicative of the old conundrum facing governments everywhere: 'how do we get our policies reflected better in a free media'? As long as the media is free to publish what it feels to be of interest to the public, politicians will never be truly satisfied. Taken in this context, the Romanian media is relatively free, certainly as free as their counterparts in the other countries of Central and Eastern Europe and perhaps even on a par with the media in certain older EU Member States.

Having considered the media in Romania let us now turn to civil society. As suggested, the media industry in Romania is competitive and, for those publications which succeed, very profitable. The basis of civil society could not be more different: charitable foundations are founded on good intentions and noble sounding projects, rather than the simple and unifying goal of selling more newspapers. It is a rather sickly element of the Romanian economy, populated by thousands of small non-governmental organizations (NGOs), the majority of which live on virtually no income whatsoever; unknown to their community and their local media. Of course there are some very strong NGOs in Romania, and each sector of civil society – in the media, environmental and cultural fields, for example – has one or two major NGOs which are publicly recognised names and sustained by a variety of funding sources. Yet for each successful NGO, there are thousands of unsustainable entities, many of which exist in name only and would be closed down if they were business enterprises or if there were a charities commission.

NGOs and a healthy civil society play an important role in modern democracies. However, each NGO should be sustained by its community, or membership, and NGOs which are totally inactive, or indeed corrupt, should be investigated and closed down. This would be in the interest of the overall health of the NGO sector, which suffers from a real image problem in Romania, where scandals about the misuse of NGO funds are fresh in peoples' minds.

Before examining the relationship between civil society and the media, however, it is important to consider the causes of the weakness of civil society in Romania. In essence, there are various reasons, none of which is unique to Romania. Indeed this phenomenon is more-or-less repeated across the region. A major factor is that civil society has emerged in the West over several hundreds of years, based on political and economic systems that have been evolving over centuries. If we take the United Kingdom as an example, modern-day civil society started its growth in the nineteenth century as a response to the excesses of the industrial revolution. For example, the philanthropist Sir James Key Shuttleworth (1804–1877) campaigned against the exploitation of children in industry and contributed to the eventual passing of the Elementary Education Act by Parliament. Other legislation of the day – such as the Factory Act and the Mines Act – would never have happened without the relentless campaigning of philanthropists. But all this happened over decades, and was driven by wealthy individuals whose desire was to improve the system from within. There are countless other examples of civil society confronting the exploitation of people and contributing towards legislative and educational solutions, and the best scenarios are when civil society emerges within the affected country as a natural humanitarian reaction to the exploitation of children, women or other groups – but all the time in keeping with the circumstances of that particular economy and culture. The problem with civil society comes when it is imposed from the outside, something which is increasingly happening.

Based on the knowledge that civil society has been a positive force for change in the West, policies have been developed to stimulate the development of civil society in countries that have emerged from various forms of totalitarian regimes, and which are discovering the opportunities and challenges offered by democracy. The phenomenon has developed in two main ways. First, there is the growth of huge 'multi-national' NGOs which have become expert at intervening in crisis situations all over the world and confidently advise governments about how to put their houses in order. They also set up 'local branches' of their NGO, often becoming the strongest NGOs in the country. Second, most major donors see the emergence of civil society in emerging economies as a strategic goal and large sums of money are made available for local NGOs. Although this policy is based on a proven tradition and the highest moral principles, it struggles due to the simple fact that in many of these 'beneficiary' countries the economy and culture is not yet ready to support a mature civil society – and in some cases new NGOs were set up simply to receive these funds. Rather than civil society being a self-sustaining movement for change, it can become nothing more than an opportunity for funding based on a declaration of good intent. The point here is that if civil society does not emerge within each individual country as a reaction to local conditions, it can go from being a genuine force of positive change to something which can be divisive and even risks corruption.

To return to Romania, the results of this externally-driven policy are clear. Prior to the 1989 revolution there was no civil society in Romania. Private organisations of any sort were banned and the first ones only emerged in 1990.

There was therefore no recent tradition of civil society, of philanthropy, of voluntary community involvement in addressing local problems. However, the communists did make great use of forced 'voluntary' labour in general and Romanians have unpleasant memories of *munca patriotic* (patriotic work) – not the most auspicious environment in which to nurture the growth of civil society. Since the early 1990s two phenomena have been evident in Romania in this area: the influx of sophisticated and experienced NGOs from other countries; and large sums of money being made available for local NGOs in the form of grants, mainly by international organisations. Although these factors have led to some very good works, they have also resulted in the distortion of Romanian civil society which has essentially become dependent on grant funds, a source of income that is unsustainable in the long term and does not require any link or support from the local community. Similarly, many grants tend to be relatively large and this can have a short term inflationary impact on salaries, something which is totally unsustainable and can be divisive in terms of community relations.

Discussions over the years with representatives of countless Romanian NGOs, despite revealing an admirable commitment and a genuine desire by many to assist the less fortunate, have frequently raised concerns about their ideas on fundraising. The EU's PHARE Programme, or other international donors, are cited with worrying regularity as the Holy Grail of their fundraising efforts but rarely do the NGOs express a desire to approach local companies, to promote their ideals and successes through the local media, or to try to expand membership. This stands in sharp contrast to the situation in most EU member states, where the majority of charitable associations are sustained by a group of supporters (usually in the form of members who pay an annual fee) who agree with the ideals and track-record of the organisation. Business and media organisations also play an important role in sustaining NGOs and, for those organisations which provide social services, local governments are emerging as an important and sustainable source of funds.

If we look at the overall relationship between civil society and the media in Romania the following observations can be made. On the positive side there has been a lot of useful coverage with regards to freedom of the media, often based on research carried out by some of the strong media NGOs. NGO activism has kept the issue of press freedom in the public domain and has brought the issue to the attention of the diplomatic community in Bucharest, as well as the EU institutions, and the resulting furore has contributed to the improvements described above. In addition, more and more media channels now see humanitarian work as a useful way of helping in crisis situations, and improving their own ratings. Recent examples include the appeal to help victims of the floods in July 2005, promoted on *Realitatea TV* in partnership with *Save the Children (Romania)*. Interesting local relationships are emerging between local NGOs and local media, a relationship of obvious interest to both parties. However, if we look at the overall quantity of coverage in the Romanian media about civil society it is clear that there is very little. Apart from a few high profile exceptions, there is not much of a relationship between civil society and the media. This is driven by the fact that civil society often lacks the skills both to understand and deal with the media. Often the media is seen as more of a threat than an opportunity – understandable considering how many bogus NGOs the press have uncovered over the years – and many NGOs don't seem to understand that a strong relationship with at least one media channel is fundamental to their success. The fact that many politicians and businessmen have their own NGOs is not seen by journalists as a mechanism to help their local communities, but as a possible means of laundering money and avoiding taxes.

The evolution of civil society has had a particular effect on child protection in Romania. The 'televised' revolution of 1989 led to an influx of international journalists to the country and more media coverage than Romania had experienced since Nadia Comăneci brought the country fame and glory at the 1976 Olympics. By early 1990 things were settling down in Romania and the media were 'shopping around' for other stories. What they discovered in Romania's child care institutions both shocked the world and led to a massive influx of grass-roots charitable initiatives from all over Europe. For much of the 1990s the emphasis was on supporting the child care institutions, even though these places were a significant part of the problem, and neither the Romanian government nor the international NGOs who were so very active in those days were able to find an effective solution to the problem. What is now clear is that the Romanian people were as shocked by the state of their child care protection system as everyone else was, and it has taken almost 15 years to come up with an effective policy that not only addresses the causes of the problem but also provides community- and family-based solutions. The new law on the *Protection and Promotion of Child Rights in Romania* came into effect in early 2005 and was based on years of efforts by successive governments, as well as much support from the PHARE programme. With this new legislation based on the rights of the children themselves, Romania now has a state-of-the-art law that is up to the highest European standards, and is faced with the challenge of implementation, a process that is being closely monitored by the Romanian press. However, the legislative situation was not always so positive. It is worth considering what happened in the 1990s, when civil society and the media came together in what they believed was the solution to the problem.

During the 1990s, inter-country adoption (ICA) came to be seen as a good way to get children out of Romania's appalling institutions and into loving families and, although accurate figures are not available, an estimated 30,000 children were adopted from Romania between 1990 and 2004. The history of adoptions from Romania can be summarised as follows: between 1991 and 1997 the process was virtually unregulated (left to the discretion of local judges); between 1997 and 2000 there were new regulations; after 2000 there was a moratorium on ICA and the flow of children almost stopped; Romania's new law on child protection, which came into effect in 2005, upholds the ban on ICA.

Civil society played an important role in this area during the period from 1997 to 2000. In 1997 the Romanian government introduced major reforms to the child protection system, which legalised the exchange of children in return for goods or hard currency. It was based on the following procedures: an institutionalised child would be declared abandoned after 6 months of no-contact with its parents; the child could then be declared eligible for adoption; one of the authorised NGOs would then facilitate the adoption process with a foreign based adoption agency. Based on a dubious 'points system', children would be allocated to those NGOs which had supported the Romanian child protection services with donations. By making donations of goods or services, often at inflated values, the NGOs would receive points, in return for which they received the right to process adoptable children.

For those wishing to speed up the flow of small children from inhospitable conditions to families overseas, this points system seemed both innovative and helpful. The setting up of social services in Romania was a process that had lagged behind as there was a real shortage of social workers in the country following Ceaușescu's banning of this profession. The points system notionally offered benefits of additional funds to social services, while taking children permanently out of the state system. In practice this reform had a deeply negative impact on Romania from a variety of points of view. According to the United Nations Convention on the Rights of the Child (UNCRC), to which the Hague Convention on Inter-Country Adoptions is subsidiary, international adoptions may only take place when local solutions cannot be found. However, when a foreign source was willing to spend hard currency on getting a child – 'prices' could be as high as US$60,000 – the temptation for underpaid local officials to bypass procedure was overwhelming. Not only were local solutions (including the baseline return of the child to its natural family wherever possible) ignored, but the institutions themselves came to be seen as processing centres for adoptable babies. This in turn stimulated some of those involved to encourage the 'abandonment' of babies and also sustained the network of decrepit child care institutions. The positive effect that ICA was supposed to have on social services never materialised, partly because most of the money involved never actually filtered through and also because the best staff from the social services would be 'headhunted' by the adoption agencies. Following the exposure of this dubious trade the Romanian government banned ICA in 2000 and has, more or less, managed to maintain the ban to the present day, despite heavy pressure to lift it.

What is particularly interesting for this analysis is the role of civil society and the media in the ICA trade. As mentioned above, a number of NGOs were authorised by the Romanian government to facilitate international adoptions in return for providing technical assistance to the social services. They were also obliged to make regular reports to the state on the fate of the individual children who ended up abroad. Over 100 NGOs were authorised. When the points system was set up, the number of international adoptions increased dramatically and many of the NGOs concerned became involved in murky financial transactions with local authorities. What is particularly telling about this story is that after 2000, when ICA was effectively put on hold, many of these NGOs simply closed up shop and disappeared. Not only did this raise questions about the capacity of NGOs to monitor individual adoption cases, which was supposedly their responsibility, but it demonstrated that many of them had no real commitment to either the development of social services in Romania or the children with which they had been involved. To this day it remains a puzzle why these NGOs do not get involved in solving the issue of local adoptions in Romania, a process that has been regulated by the new law on child rights but is still dysfunctional. There is still a problem of child abandonment in Romanian maternity hospitals, yet there appears to be little evidence of local NGOs providing the sort of assistance they were so keen to promise during the 1997 to 2000 period. The *Jurnalul Naţional* newspaper seems to be more interested in doing something than most NGOs (with the notable exception of *Save the Children*).

Before considering the role of the media in the ICA process, it is important to understand the role of the international lobby for the resumption of ICA from Romania. Although ICA was banned in 2000, successive Romanian governments gave the impression that it would eventually be repealed, and this is the message that has gone out to adoption agencies all over the world. The country that adopted the most children from Romania was the United States, location of the strongest and best organised ICA lobby. There are also strong ICA lobbies in France, Spain, Israel and Italy and together they apply considerable pressure on the Romanian government. In the United States, there is a Congressional Committee on ICA and over 40 members of Congress signed a letter to President Băsescu in 2005 saying, 'For these children, international adoption is their only chance to find a permanent and loving home'. Unfortunately the Romanian government's formal and accurate reply to the erroneous statements from this Congressional commission was not accepted by the commission chairman.

What role does the press play in this lobby for the resumption of ICA? To be fair, the international media have generally played a straight game regarding the ICA issue and their coverage of the progress made in reforming Romania's child welfare system has been fair, albeit rather understated. There has been a lot less negative news from Romania in 2005. However, what is becoming increasingly clear is that many NGOs have a vested interest in continuing to portray Romania as a basket case, where the children are still languishing in appalling institutions and where nothing has changed since the early 1990s, as this helps to provide the context for their own fundraising efforts. This image is fed to the media and while the respectable international media do not really buy it, the local media (i.e. the local paper where that particular NGO is based) are happy to use the old stereotypes. Negative stories, based on local families 'doing good' in Romania, are particularly common in the United States.

There was a more challenging article which appeared in the spring of 2005 in the *International Herald Tribune,* an article that was reproduced in *The New York Times* and other American publications. It described the new law on child rights as being well meaning but ineffective and portrayed a worrying picture of institutionalised children in Romania: 'There are close to 10,000 children abandoned at hospitals each year in Romania, according to a new study by UNICEF, and up to 50,000 children in the care of the state'.[4] The Romanian newspaper *Jurnalul Naţional* also made good use of this figure of 10,000 abandoned babies in a series of double page spreads on the issue.

These figures seemed wrong and were subsequently investigated. According to the Romanian Government's National Authority for the Protection of Child Rights (NAPCR) there were a total of 4,600 children left in Romanian hospitals in 2004 and over 50% of these were subsequently re-united with their own parents, some within a matter of days. Also, according to NAPCR, there were a total of 83,000 children in state care in 2004. Out of this total, over 50,000 children were with foster or extended families. The authenticity of the NAPCR figures and the appropriateness of their data gathering techniques were also checked. It was found that NAPCR obtain their official figures from the social and health services in each of Romania's 41 counties, whereas UNICEF had based their estimates on just two regions (neither of

---

[4] UNICEF, *The Situation of Child Abandonment in Romania* (New York: UNICEF, 2005)

which were identified in the study). *The New York Times* subsequently spotted this discrepancy in an article on Romanian children in September 2005.[5]

In conclusion, it is clear that there is a disparity between the relative health of the Romanian media and civil society. Despite inauspicious beginnings, the media has slowly but surely been evolving into an impressive force, which will hopefully continue to develop and mature, maintaining the current levels of independence and cheekiness – which is after all a good litmus test of a free media. In contrast, there are good grounds to be concerned about the state of civil society in Romania where its development has been distorted by unfortunate overdependence on grant funds from large international donors. This is to the detriment of creating genuinely broad-based civil society bodies with popular support in which members are linked to the organisation through subscriptions. This would provide the large degree of stability and longevity that independent NGOs require for successful development. Not only would the evolution of an increasingly robust civil society in Romania be a considerable boon to society at large and of benefit to any government in power, but it would also provide the strength and confidence needed to stand up in the face of those who would seek to devalue Romania's achievements and to undermine her own laws. For despite the false image of a backward country on the periphery of Europe that persists in some sections of the international media, Romania has come on by leaps and bounds in the past fifteen years. Her progress must be commended and supported, and I look forward to the day when she takes up her seat at the EU's top table.

---

[5] 'Romania Seeks to Reverse a Harsh Era for Its Children', *The New York Times*, 25 September 2005, p. 3.

CHAPTER SEVEN

Romania's Accession Negotiations with the EU: A Chief Negotiator's Perspective

Leonard Orban

Romania officially opened accession negotiations with the European Union (EU) in February 2000 following a decision of the Helsinki European Council in December 1999. With the EU pursuing a flexible, multi-speed accession process, the objective was to ensure that the pace of the negotiations would reflect Romania's preparations for membership. At the same time, Romania was part of a 'comprehensive, evolutive and inclusive' process including ten countries from Central and Eastern Europe as well as Malta and Cyprus. All these 'candidate' countries participated in the process on an equal footing and all were destined to join the EU on the basis of the same criteria.

The pace of negotiations was determined not only by the commitments made by the individual candidates, but also by the correct transposition and implementation of the *acquis*, including effective and efficient application through appropriate administrative and judicial structures. Negotiations with Romania were completed in December 2004 when the European Council noted that the progress made in implementing the *acquis* made possible the formal conclusion of all negotiation chapters. It also decided that Romania's Accession Treaty should be signed in April 2005.

What follows is an assessment of Romania's progress through the accession negotiations that highlights some of the key challenges that the Romanian negotiating team had to face and how these were resolved. It begins, however, with brief forays into Romania-EU relations prior to 1999 and the political background to the accession negotiations.

ROMANIA – EU RELATIONS

Relations between Romania and the EU have a special history, dating back to the 1960s, when several technical agreements in the field of agricultural and industrial products were concluded. Later on, in 1980, an agreement on trade in industrial goods was concluded. Among other things, this established a Joint Commission between Romania and the then European Economic Community (EEC). Romania was therefore the first Central and Eastern European (CEE) country to recognize *de facto* the EEC.

Following the fall of the Ceauşescu regime in 1989, Romania sought closer ties with the EU. On 1 February 1993, it signed a Europe Agreement with the EU, acquiring with its entry into force in February 1995 the status of 'associate' of the EU. The Europe Agreement was a key stage on Romania's road to accession. It involved the liberalization of trade between Romania and the EU, the extension of the other freedoms on which the EU is based, and the promotion of economic and financial cooperation. The implementation of the Europe Agreement as well as 'structured dialogue' with the EU contributed to a gradual *rapprochement* with and integration into the EU as a community of values and interests.

The process was intensified following the 1997 Luxembourg European Council's decisions to embark on an all-inclusive and evolving enlargement process and formally launch an accession process in March 1998 with all applicant countries, including Romania. Subsequently, on 13 October 1999, the European Commission recommended to the EU's member states that accession negotiations with Romania, Slovakia, Latvia, Lithuania, Bulgaria and Malta, known as the *Helsinki six*, be opened. They duly were in February 2000 following a decision of the Helsinki European Council in December 1999 which also reaffirmed the inclusive nature of the accession process.

THE POLITICAL BACKGROUND TO THE ACCESSION NEGOTIATIONS

Romania's process of accession to the EU can be correctly understood if assessed as an historic opportunity and as the biggest modernization challenge since the Second World War. On the former, the opportunity existed to become part of an inclusive and evolutive accession process involving ten CEE applicant countries, Malta and Cyprus that would result in Romania being fully integrated in a community based on the principles and values of democracy, respect for fundamental human rights and freedoms, the rule of law and a market economy. On the second, the challenge lay in speeding up economic reform, adopting and implementation EC legislation, and strengthening domestic institutional capacities, so that Romania could catch up with other candidate countries more advanced in this process.

Historic Opportunity

Even though the main requirement imposed on a candidate country wishing to join the EU is to promote domestic reforms so as to meet the accession criteria laid down by the European Council, notably at Copenhagen in 1993, and assume certain obligations before being admitted to the EU, the dynamics of the fifth enlargement were not driven solely by the state of preparedness of the candidate countries for membership. Various geopolitical and strategic factors also influenced the process.

Romania's relations with the EU have developed since 1989 within the general framework of the EU's relations with the CEE countries. Romania partially owes its current position in the enlargement process to the dynamics of this broader context. Moreover, Romania's position has also been influenced by external events, like political developments in the Balkan region and the Kosovo conflict in 1999. Also, even though Romania was less prepared than other candidate countries, most EU member states wished to avoid new notions of 'ins' and 'outs' and new differentiations in the EU's relations with the CEE countries. Excluding the least prepared countries from the process could have undermined their domestic economic and political reform processes. Romania seized these opportunities and benefited from the response of the EU to pursue an 'inclusive and evolutive' accession process involving all the CEE countries.

The Biggest Challenge After the Second World War

Romania, alongside the other CEE countries started a colossal societal reform process at the beginning of the 1990s aimed at bringing its society and economy over time up to levels comparable with those in the western part of Europe. This process of modernization after the communist period was heavily influenced in Romania by external factors.

Currently, Romania has behind it a decade of change that nobody would have dreamt of only 15 years ago. Moreover, the dynamics of societal change have never been so profound. Accession to the EU has been the biggest stimulus and challenge for Romania over the last 15 years. Indeed, the process of accession to the EU went hand in hand with the process of modernizing the country both economically and politically. In doing so, the EU aimed to achieve stable institutions guaranteeing democracy, the rule of law, human rights and the protection of minorities and the development of market economy.

The fall of the Berlin Wall was therefore the start of a process aimed at furthering the dream of the founders of the EEC, as stated in the preamble to its founding treaty: 'an ever closer union among the peoples of Europe'. Such a union of peoples, such a historical process of integration has been the only way to overcome the painful experiences of the past.

The fifth enlargement: principles of the negotiations

Accession negotiations determine the conditions under which applicant countries will join the EU. For Romania, the negotiations were conducted in bilateral accession conferences with the EU member states on the basis of 31 chapters of the *acquis*. Negotiating sessions were held either at the level of ministers or deputies. Progress in negotiations depended on the degree of preparation and the complexity of the issues to be resolved. During its accession negotiations, Romania observed the following principles, as announced at the beginning of this process:

- to proceed in good faith and to conduct the accession negotiations on the principles and procedures as defined by the EU in its opening statement for accession negotiations;
- to progress in fully complying with the accession criteria as defined by the Copenhagen and Madrid European Councils within a framework of economic and social convergence;
- to observe strictly the provisions of the Europe Agreement, of the Accession Partnership, including the intermediate priorities, and of other bilateral agreements between Romania and the EU;
- to be ready for accession on 1 January 2007;

Furthermore, Romania committed itself:

- to settle any border disputes in the framework of either Stability Pact procedures or by means of dispute settlement methods laid down in the United Nations Charter;
- to align progressively, in the perspective of accession, its policies and positions to those adopted by the EU and its member states.

The fifth enlargement: Romania's negotiation strategy

In order to open accession negotiation for each chapter, two conditions had to be fulfilled: a minimum necessary level of adoption and implementation of the *acquis*, together with the presentation of a Position Paper that should reflect properly the situation and that should present future programs for fulfilling the requirements of accession. Chapters were opened for negotiations following receipt by the EU of the negotiation position of the applicant country and a unanimous decision of the Council on a draft common negotiating position

The provisional closure of the negotiation of one chapter required transposition and implementation of the *acquis*, including the conclusion of negotiations on transitional periods, derogations or technical arrangements, if necessary, and satisfactory answers to EU questions. The EU, while accepting provisional closure of a chapter, insisted, however, on the global character of the negotiations: i.e. *nothing is agreed until everything is agreed*. Hence chapters could always be reopened.

The pace of negotiations was determined by the correct transposition and implementation of the *acquis*, including effective and efficient application through appropriate administrative and judicial structures. The period 2000–2004 represented basically the period when Romania initiated the most important administrative and legislative reforms necessary for building its institutional capacity and for coordinating the process of its internal preparations for accession.

2000 – 2004: FROM A SLUGGISH BEGINNING TO A 'GENUINE MARATHON'

By the end of 2000, Romania had officially transmitted to the EU Council position papers for only 13 negotiating chapters. Of these, nine had been opened and six provisionally closed. These were considered to be the 'easy' chapters. Other candidates had opened and closed more chapters. Consequently, by December 2000, Romania was already lagging behind other candidate countries, including those that had started negotiations at the same time as Romania. For example, Latvia, Lithuania and Slovakia presented their position papers for all negotiating chapters at the beginning of negotiations. Bulgaria too had presented significantly more position papers during 2000. That Romania was lagging behind was due to various factors, not least the economic situation in the country, its structural complexity compared to the other smaller candidate countries, and the state of Romania's internal preparations for accession.

Indeed, little progress in the adoption and putting into force of the *acquis*, which were essential factors for the advancement of accession negotiation, had been made prior to 2000. Furthermore, the team in charge of Romania's negotiations with the EU – the National Delegation for Negotiations – was created relatively late and the institutional process of internal coordination only began at the same time as the opening of negotiations. The Ministry of European Integration was especially created in 2001 in order to ensure the coordination of Romania's preparations for accession to the EU, as well as the coordination of the accession negotiations.

2001: A Quantitative Approach

During 2001 negotiation strategy focused on a quantitative approach, analysing the whole *acquis*. The process was inwardly orientated with the National Delegation for Negotiations focusing on consultations with the social partners, political parties, national parliamentary committees and civil society. The strategic objective for the year was to draw up and send to Brussels, by the end of 2001, the position papers for all outstanding negotiating chapters. The fulfilment of this objective would allow Romania to enter into the substance of negotiations and facilitate the speeding up of the opening and provisional closure of chapters. 2001 was also significant in that it saw a new dimension added to preparations for accession: cooperation and communication with EU member and other candidate states, with a special focus on those member states holding the Presidency of the Council of the EU. Another important development in 2001 was the beginning of the process of monitoring commitments made during negotiations. By the end of 2001, the position papers for 29 negotiating chapters had been officially communicated to the EU. Romania had also opened 17 chapters. Of these, nine had been provisionally closed.

2002: A Qualitative Approach

During 2002, the negotiation strategy focused on a qualitative approach, comprising arguments for derogations, transitional periods, and technical arrangements and on providing the supplementary information requested by the EU in its Common Positions. The main objectives for the year were to open all negotiating chapters, to strictly monitor the commitments taken during negotiations and to enforce cooperation and communication with member and candidate states.

The European Council in Copenhagen, in December 2002, represented an important moment for Romania as it set 2007 as the goal for accession. Setting a date and adopting a new 'road map', together with supplementary financial aid, represented substantial advancements in the dynamics of accession negotiations. Added to this, negotiations were provisionally closed for seven more chapters. Also, by the end of 2002, Romania had opened negotiations on 30 chapters, out of which 16 chapters were now provisionally closed.

2003: Entering the Tough Negotiations

2003 saw Romania negotiate some of the most difficult chapters. These covered large amounts of the *acquis* and required the harmonization of Romanian economic policies with those of the EU. The strategic objective for 2003 focused on substantial advancement regarding the provisional closure of the chapters, with an emphasis on the chapters related to the internal market. There was also a focus on the monitoring of commitments and the strengthening of cooperation and communication with the member and candidate states.

The progress registered by Romania in the process of internal preparation was recognized by the European Council in Thessaloniki in June 2003 and again in Brussels in December 2003.These reaffirmed the common objective of the EU(25) to admit Romania as a member of the EU on 1 January 2007. Furthermore, the European Council announced its support for finalizing accession negotiations in 2004 and signing the Accession Treaty in early 2005.

In accordance with the strategy set out at the beginning of 2003, Romania focused on submitting supplementary information, as requested by the EU, which allowed the advancement in the negotiations. By the end of 2003, 22 negotiating chapters had been provisionally closed.

2004: The 'Negotiation Marathon' for Romania

Romania braced itself for a genuine 'negotiation marathon' between January and mid-December 2004. From a negotiator's point of view, 2004 was the most difficult year in Romania's accession to the EU. First, it was not the best period for finalizing EU talks, given the nervousness created by the uncertainties surrounding the negotiations on a European Constitution. Second, debates were still ongoing about whether Turkey should be offered accession. Third, difficulties in digesting a large group of ten new member states following enlargement on 1 May added to the trend of euroscepticism in Europe.

For Romania, 2004 involved negotiating the most difficult chapters, including justice and home affairs, competition, environment. It also saw negotiations on the financial package governing the accession of Romania and Bulgaria to the EU. And domestically, 2004 was a year in which Romania not only accelerated the adoption and implementation of the *acquis* for the opened chapters but also strove to fulfil its commitments related to the previously closed chapters.

The pressure on Romania was even greater after the accession of the eight CEE countries, Cyprus and Malta on 1 May 2004. Indeed, greater attention was focused on Romania as an individual candidate due to the fewer number of candidates. Its preparations for membership were put under the spotlight more than before. The European Parliament became particularly vocal in its demands that Romania meet its obligations.

All these factors contributed to the speeding up of the accession negotiations in 2004. After the European Commission's Regular Report in October 2004, Romania finalized the last and most difficult three chapters in the December. The chapters were the same three that those CEE countries involved in the 2004 enlargement had concluded last in 2002: competition, environment and justice and home affairs.

THE MOST DIFFICULT CHAPTERS IN THE NEGOTIATIONS

Unlike former accession rounds, the EU's fifth enlargement included negotiations on new and difficult policy areas like monetary union, justice and home affairs and security and defence policy. The negotiations and conditions imposed by the EU were tough. Within the negotiation process, tough bargaining took place over financing, the free movement of labour and market access.

Accession implies Romania's full acceptance and effective implementation of the actual and potential rights and obligations concerning to the *acquis* and the EU's institutional framework. Romania, like other candidate countries, has to apply this as it stands at the time of accession.

Chapter 4: Free Movement of Capital

The first difficult chapter negotiated by Romania was Chapter 4 – Free movement of capital, which marked the opening of the negotiations on the four freedoms on which the EU is based. Furthermore, the negotiation on this chapter had for the first time a horizontal approach, due to the implications of this chapter in many other fields. The negotiation was opened in spring 2001 and provisionally closed in June 2003. The most difficult aspects concerned the motivation behind the requested transition periods on the acquisition of agricultural land, forests and forestry land by EU and European Economic Area (EEA) citizens. Due to the lack of impact studies and the state of internal preparations, Romania lagged behind in the presentation of its position paper. All other candidate countries opened the negotiations on this chapter in 1999–2000 and provisionally closed them in 2001, although Poland only closed the chapter in 2002 due to political and historical reasons.

Negotiations on the free movement of capital were politically sensitive since property rights regarding agricultural land were only relatively recently re-established in Romania after a long period of state ownership and complete state control of land use. The extension of the right to own property on land to foreigners upon accession would have resulted in an increase in land prices in Romania and would have created distortions on the land market. These would have lead to social problems at regional and national level. During the negotiation process, Romania reduced its request for a transitional period from 15 to seven years and accepted the EU position on this issue. At the end of the negotiations on this chapter, Romania obtained two transitional arrangements. The first is a five-year transitional period allowing for existing restrictions on the acquisition of land for secondary residences to be maintained. EU and EEA citizens residing in Romania are not, however, covered by the restrictions. The second transitional arrangement concerns the maintenance for seven years of restrictions on the acquisition of agricultural and forestry land. Self-employed farmers who are nationals of the member states and residing in Romania are excluded from its scope.

Chapter 6: Competition Policy

This chapter was opened in November 2000 and it was provisionally closed in December 2004. The conclusion of negotiations was not only conditioned by the existence of a transposed legal framework, but mainly by the appropriate implementation of the transposed legislation (i.e. Romania's enforcement record). For Romania, the most difficult part of the negotiation process was implementation of the *acquis* regarding state aids, particularly in the steel sector, due to the large number of restructuring and privatization cases. For the conclusion of the negotiations on this chapter, the negotiation team had to convince all domestic institutions involved in this process to observe the competition rules, in accordance with the *acquis*. Hence, regarding the steel sector, Romania is committed to: not granting or paying any state aids to the steel mills covered by the National Restructuring Strategy from 1 January 2005 to 31 December 2008 (i.e. the end of the restructuring period); respecting the amounts of state aid established in the context of Protocol 2 of the Europe Agreement; and respecting the total capacity reductions for finished products. To this end, Romania presented a detailed timetable of the expected dates for the cessation of production and for the dismantling and destruction of installations. The final destruction will be notified to the Commission.

During the negotiations, Romania obtained three transitional arrangements. The first two cover the phasing-out of incompatible fiscal aid. In the case of aid for undertakings that, under the Law on Free Trade Areas, signed commercial contracts with the Free Trade Areas Administrations before 1 July 2002, the deadline is 31 December 2011. In the case of undertakings that, under the Government Emergency Ordinance on Deprived Areas, were granted a permanent investor certificate before 1 July 2003, the deadline is 31 December 2010. In both cases such state aid is granted for regional investments and the aid net intensity must not exceed the rate of 50% net grant equivalent (up to 65% for SMEs provided that the total net aid intensity does not exceed 75%). In the motor vehicle sector, the total aid may not exceed a maximum of 30% of the eligible investments costs. The third transitional arrangement concerns the restructuring of the steel sector by the end of 2008. In addition, a specific safeguard that will allow the envisaged date of accession to be postponed by one year to January 2008 was also negotiated. Any serious shortcoming regarding competition policy, especially as regards Romania's state aid enforcement record, observed in the 2005 and 2006 European Commission's Regular Report, can activate this delay. Activation will require a decision by the Council acting by qualified majority on the basis of a Commission recommendation.

Chapter 22: Environment

This chapter was opened in March 2002 and provisionally closed in November 2004. Because of the complexity of the *acquis* in this field and its horizontal implications, alignments to EU environmental norms have required profound transformation in all sectors of the economy. These have proved especially challenging in a country with no tradition in environmental protection. Numerous meetings were therefore held between industry representatives and the central administration in order to raise awareness of the new environmental requirements. Following these meetings, industry representatives provided the necessary arguments for the transitional arrangements requested by Romanian negotiations.

Another challenging aspect for the Romanian negotiators was the lack of a collective environmental conscience. At the beginning of the negotiations on the environment chapter there was no real understanding of the need to conserve the country's natural heritage. There was also no public environmental education and information that could facilitate the absorption and under-standing of the environmental need to ensure the quality of life of current and future generations.

The transitional periods granted during the negotiations relate to 11 directives and will last for up to twelve years. Romania therefore has:

- between one and three years to comply with the requirements of the directive on emissions of volatile organic compounds resulting from the transport and distribution of petrol;

- between three and five years to reach the recovery/recycling targets for plastic, glass and wood provided by the directive on packaging and packaging waste;
- between one and two years to comply with the requirements on waste incineration;
- between three and nine years to ensure that 130 waste landfills comply with the *acquis*;
- two years to reach the collection, recycling and reuse targets for electric and electronic waste;
- between five and nine years to apply in full provisions relating to waste transport;
- between nine and twelve years for complete application of requirements in the field of waste water treatment;
- between four and nine years to reach quality objectives of drinking water;
- three years for dangerous substances (Hexachlorobenzene (HCB), Hexachlorobutadiene (HCBD), 1,2 – Dichloroethane, Trichloroethilene, Trichlorobenzene, for 21 industrial units from the chemical industry (inorganic, organic, rubber, petrochemical sector, pulp and paper); Cadmium and Mercury, for 27 industrial units; Lindane, for 3 industrial units;
- eight years and two months to ensure that 195 industrial installations comply with the provisions of the directive on industrial pollution prevention and control;
- six years to comply with the limit values for SO_2 (34 installations), NO_x (69 installations), dust (26 installations) and one year for NO_x (6 installations).

Chapter 24: Cooperation in the Field of Justice and Home Affairs

This chapter was opened in April 2002 and provisionally closed in December 2004. The main difficulty in negotiating EU policies on Justice and Home Affairs (JHA) consisted in the fact that it touched upon some of the most sensitive questions for public opinion, both in the EU and in Romania. JHA policies aim to maintain and further develop the EU as an area of freedom, security and justice. Thus, following negotiations on this chapter, Romania must respect hundreds of commitments resulting from the 13 areas covered by the JHA. This has involved a profound reform of the administrative, judicial, and policing structures in the country and a most thorough reconsideration of not only state structures and organisation but also of mentalities within the public administration and the judicial system. It basically involved rearranging the fundamentals of the state on a new basis, as the JHA chapter crossed with many issues found under the political criteria heading, such as combating corruption and reforming state institutions.

Unlike in the case of the other negotiation chapters no transition periods were sought. This is because Romania focused on finding ways to build up confidence among the member states in its capacity to implement the *acquis*. On issues such as border control, illegal migration, drugs trafficking and money laundering, organised crime, police and judicial cooperation, data protection and the mutual recognition of court judgments, there was a need to ensure that Romania was equipped to meet required and acceptable standards of implementation. In many cases, institutions and structures had to be built from scratch and staff had to be recruited and trained to help meet new commitments, which in many cases did not exist before. Furthermore, the establishment of an independent, reliable and efficient judiciary and a re-organisation of the police have been of paramount importance.

Romania is nevertheless subject to general and specific safeguard clauses in the JHA field. A first covers judicial co-operation in civil and criminal matters and states that in cases of inadequate transposition or implementation of any parts of the relevant *acquis* during the first three years after accession, the application of these provisions may be temporarily suspended in respect of new member states. This clause was also included in the Accession Treaty with the first ten candidate countries. A second and specific safeguard clause can be activated by the Council acting by a qualified majority and allows for the entry of Romania to the EU to be postponed by one year in case of unsatisfactory progress in certain fields of JHA . The clause covers matters related to the implementation of the Schengen Action Plan, the modernization of external border controls, the development of a feasible, integrated strategy and action plan for the reform of the judicial system, intensification of the fight against corruption (especially high-level corruption), the assurance of a clear legal framework of cooperation between the gendarmerie and police, as well as developing and implementing a coherent multi-annual strategy for combating crime.

BIGGEST CHALLENGES FROM A CHIEF NEGOTIATOR'S PERSPECTIVE

Romania's process of accession to the EU was particularly complex and difficult. During this process, Romania had to overcome intricate internal and external challenges. Five stand out. First, Romania was a late starter compared to the other CEE countries and had to cope with a difficult macroeconomic environment. As regards the economy, it is worth recalling that Romania's former leader, Nicolae Ceaușescu , wanted to pay back all foreign debt. This happened over a period lasting almost ten years in the 1980s. By 1989 Romania had paid back around $10 billion. In doing so, however, the modernization of the economy was sacrificed. Although Romania ended up with no foreign debt, it had forgone an opportunity to invest in modern industrial technologies. Following the events of 1989, economic modernization was once again neglected as attention shifted to property ownership. Another ten years of under investment followed. In fact, Romania has only really started to modernize its economy in the last few years, notably with the help of greenfield investments. The period of transition at the beginning of the 1990s was therefore also somehow a period of stand-by in economic terms. Also, between 1996 and 2000, when most of the other candidate countries were preparing for accession to the EU, Romania was going through four years of economic recession. Internally, the country had to cope with a difficult macroeconomic environment. In 2000 the inflation rate was 45%, and the rate of recession between 1997 and 2000 was 13%. This trend was reversed in 2001, when the economy grew by 5%.

Second, Romania entered the intricate process of preparing for accession to the EU almost unprepared. The administration only really appreciated the complexity of the process from the second half of 2001 onwards. By then most of the other candidate countries had already drawn up the necessary documents for their negotiations with the EU. Moreover, before 2001, the Romanian administration did not have the capacity to carry out impact studies or solid assessments to serve as a basis for the position papers submitted during negotiations. As a consequence, decisions on certain negotiating chapters were taken without knowing all the implications.

Third, Romania almost missed the first stage in the accession process: the screening process involving the analytical examination of the 31 chapters of the *acquis*. In April 1998, Romania, jointly with Latvia, Lithuania, Bulgaria and Slovakia, started the general multilateral screening process of domestic legislation for its conformity with the *acquis*. The stage of screening is fundamental as it provides relevant information on whether the candidate country can accept relevant provisions of the *acquis*; whether it intends to request transitional arrangements; whether it has already adopted the laws necessary to comply with the *acquis*, and if not when it intends to adopt such laws; whether it possesses the administrative structure and other capacities needed to adopt and implement EU laws properly and, if not, when these structures will be put in place. Unlike other candidate countries, Romania did not take full advantage of the screening process, whose findings should have served as a basis for the accession negotiations. Instead, it approached the process more like an intellectual exercise than as a pre-negotiation stage.

Fourth, the team in charge of Romania's negotiations with the EU was created relatively late and the institutional process of internal coordination only began at the same time as the opening of negotiations. The team became fully operative by the end of 2001, combining a few senior experts with wide experience in the field of European affairs and a number of very young experts. Not only was the negotiating process tough at the beginning, it was also a *learning-by-doing process*. Nevertheless, the negotiation team strengthened, rapidly achieving the necessary technical expertise and ensuring the highest political involvement in the accession negotiation. By the end of 2004, the negotiation team had gained the respect of all the institutions of the Romanian central administration.

Fifth, it was not easy to handle a two-level negotiation process. Negotiations had to be conducted with, on the one hand, the EU member states and, on the other, the domestic actors (institutions of the central administration, local administration, multinational companies). Internally, under difficult social and economic circumstances, the Romanian negotiation team had to fight with fears that arise whenever a country embarks upon the process of European integration. One was the fear that the country would lose its sovereignty to a centralist decision-making process that would ignore its interests. Altogether, the opposition against the process of accession to the EU was not strong in Romania and did not succeed in crystallizing, not even at the end of the process. The involvement of the business community was initially low. At the beginning only multinational companies sought to influence the evolution of the process. By the end of 2003–2004 Romanian business interests had become far more involved.

Furthermore, although Romania's accession talks were part of a wider accession process comprising ten CEE countries as well as Cyprus and Malta, there were changes in the negotiating process with Romania. In light of the experience of the negotiations with the first 10 candidate countries, the European Commission's assessments became tougher on sensitive issues. The opening or closure of a chapter for negotiations was only recommended by the European Commission provided that Romania was well prepared or had fulfilled specific benchmarks. Depending on the chapter, benchmarks referred to legislative alignment or to a satisfactory track record in implementation of the *acquis* demonstrating the existence of an adequate administrative and judicial capacity.

CONCLUSION

This assessment of Romania's progress through the accession negotiations has tried to highlight the most difficult challenges that the Romanian negotiation team had to face both internally and externally and how these were surpassed. Even though Romania was a late starter compared to the other CEE countries, had to overcome difficult social and economic circumstances, and did not take full advantage of the pre-negotiation stage, it was able to close the gap and the negotiation team strengthened rapidly, achieving the necessary technical expertise and respect from EU and national central administration institutions. Despite domestic and external difficulties, Romania concentrated all its efforts in order to meet the criteria required by the *acquis* and was capable of concluding the 'negotiation marathon' by mid-December 2004. Considering the pace of progress made by Romania in the fields identified by the European Commission as the most sensitive, Romania will be ready for accession on 1 January 2007. All the Romanian institutions and the entire strategy for internal preparation for accession to the EU have as strategic objective Romania's accession to the EU in 2007.

Fully-fledged membership of the EU will not only be beneficial for Romania, but also for the entire Union. This is because enlargement represents a win-win situation with mutual benefits for all involved. From the economic point of view, Romania's membership will be beneficial for the entire EU as it will extend the Internal Market and will increase the number of consumers by 22 million; it will provide a common regulatory framework for European companies through its level playing field and a more transparent and predictable business environment: and it could facilitate the expansion of European companies towards Western Balkans. From the geostrategic and geopolitical point of view, Romania's membership will accomplish the project of the fifth wave of enlargement in a united Europe without new division lines. It will increase the international political credibility of the EU as an actor capable of finalizing assumed objectives and it will lead to the further stabilization of the region, especially of the Western Balkans, by means of two success stories: Romania and Bulgaria.

Romania in the European Union

CHAPTER EIGHT

The European Union and Romania: Interests and Aspirations

Lazăr Comănescu

Romania's interests and aspirations relative to European Union (EU) membership cannot be dissociated from the political developments in Europe following the Second World War, the fall of the Iron curtain and the end of communism in 1989, as well as Romania's place in the history of the European continent. Less than 12 months away from accession, the present outlook on EU membership is also the result of a continuous process of learning and adaptation of expectations. Unfolding during the last 15 years, this process has been modulated by domestic reforms and transformations, as well as unprecedented developments at EU level.

Although the prospect of EU accession was offered several years later, 1989 can be considered as the starting point on the road leading to an EU of 25, soon 27 members. The fall of the communist regimes resulted, as a first reaction, in a strong desire, all across Central and Eastern Europe, to join European and international organisations. Romania adopted this approach as a means of facilitating reintegration into the world economic and political community, as well as a way of breaking with the past and of distancing itself from the then Soviet sphere of influence. Accession to the Council of Europe in October 1993, for example, besides the practical benefits, had also a symbolic value, the affirmation of independence and sovereignty, as well as proof of the success of the transition process.

Reintegrating the democratic (Western) values and, therefore, joining the Western economic, political and security institutions which had contributed decisively to the promotion and strengthening of these values became, after 1990, one of the main foreign policy goals of the Central and Eastern European

(CEE) countries. Romania was no exception in this respect. The immediate, beneficial, effect was a process of rapid opening up of the economies of the former COMECON countries and consolidation of their democratic institutions. The EU accession criteria set out in Copenhagen in June 1993 also acted as a beacon and driver for the profound political and economic reforms that have taken place in the CEE countries throughout the 1990s. But what exactly prompted these countries, not long before on the eastern side of the iron curtain to embark on this sinuous journey, in uncharted territory, that was meant to lead, in the end, to full membership of the EU?

The, primary, overarching motivation for Romania's application, in June 1995, to join the EU was one of a historical and emotional nature: 'the return to Europe', and regaining its 'rightful place in the European family' were among the most frequently used arguments. EU accession was thus seen as part of an historic process in which the CEE countries would overcome a division of the continent which had lasted for more than 40 years and join the area of peace, stability and prosperity created during this period.

Although the decisions taken by the Copenhagen European Council in 1993 clearly opened the way to EU enlargement towards the 'associated countries of central and eastern Europe', it was not clear at that time what the precise geographical scope of this enlargement would be. It is worth remembering, in this context, that historical and geographical reasons were often used in promoting and arguing in favour of EU membership. In Romania, for example, considerable energy was directed towards stressing the message that the country was geographically situated in the centre of Europe (which, technically, was not a difficult task at all). In a period perceived as full of uncertainties, the concern, justified or not, was that arbitrary historical, cultural or geographical criteria might be used by the EU in determining its future eastern borders. Being considered part of Central Europe was thus seen as an additional, convincing proof of Romania's European past and a guarantee of its future in Europe. On the other hand, there were views according to which belonging to anything else but Central Europe could mean, in the eyes of EU decision makers and public opinion, association either with the instability of the Balkans or the developments taking place in the former Soviet space.

To add to the feeling of uncertainty, the undeniable challenges of enlargement towards Central and Eastern Europe were prompting academic debates on various alternatives of partial participation in EU activities and policies, as an end objective. These 'solutions', leading only to a strengthened relationship with the EU were, however, discarded, as they were running counter to the main rationale of the CEE countries' desire to join the EU: that of dismantling all barriers and of becoming, once again, a full part of Europe. For the CEE countries, equal treatment with the EU member states was a matter of political principle and not simply a way of targeting specific economic benefits.

It was only in 1997, with the decisions taken by the European Council in Luxemburg, that the format of the EU's future eastern enlargement became clearer, although the timing of accession was still uncertain and closely linked to the degree of preparedness of both sides: the CEE counties and the EU. Thus, the enlargement landmarks were only progressively revealed, every two or three years: in Helsinki in 1999, in Copenhagen in 2002 and in Brussels in 2004.

One should also remember that, in the mid-1990s when EU membership applications were being submitted, it was not at all clear what would or should come first: EU or NATO membership. In parallel with accession to the EU, NATO membership was also one of the main foreign policy goals of the CEE countries. Accession to NATO can be seen as a natural reflex following the fall of the Berlin Wall. Returning to Europe, in its multifaceted political, economic and security dimensions, necessarily implied membership of the organization that had been the guarantor of Western Europe's defence during the last 50 years. The perceived need for a security umbrella provided by the 'right side' is understandable enough. But NATO membership also meant much more than hard security guarantees. It also meant dropping another anchor in the Euro-Atlantic community of values, peace and prosperity, the place where the CEE countries felt they belonged. Security cannot be the only explanation of the desire to join NATO in the same way as economic prosperity cannot be the main reason for the EU's attractiveness. An argument in this sense is that EU membership itself can be perceived as offering an implicit security guarantee. Although the present EU treaties do not contain formal mutual defence obligations, the emphasis on solidarity and 'ever-closer' integration within the EU, as well as the degree of interdependence reached, can be considered as an assurance that EU member states, most of which are NATO members, will not remain passive if a fellow member state is threatened. Moreover, the Constitutional Treaty will, after entering (if ever) into force, transform this implicit obligation into an explicit Treaty provision, with Article I-41(7) on mutual assistance in the case of armed aggression.

On the domestic side, as the preparations for EU accession progressed and as understanding of the workings of the EU deepened, the uncontested overall political goal of EU membership started to be accompanied by a progressively clearer image of what membership entails in terms of benefits and obligations. As accession day approaches and as information campaigns intensify, the issue of what to expect from EU membership becomes more and more present in the public domain, in parallel with an increased interest of those directly concerned, such as the ordinary citizen or the business community.

Although they were secondary to the purely political arguments and did not occupy a prominent place in the political discourse or policy documents, potential economic benefits through increased trade, investment and EU financial transfers were undeniably present among the background expectations linked to EU membership. When talking about the economic benefits of enlargement, however, it is not always easy to draw a clear line between the benefits already incurred during the accession process (as an effect of the Europe Agreement, candidate status and the opening of negotiations) and those benefits resulting directly from membership. One can, for example, easily calculate the net inflow of EU funds that accompany accession.[1] However, they represent only part of a much more comprehensive set of benefits which go far beyond the economic or financial ones.

It is common knowledge that the business community bases its investment decisions on the conditions on the ground, as well as on its expectations for the future. Thus, the clearer the accession calendar, the more 'interesting' a candidate country becomes. As in the case of the other candidate countries, Romania had a justified interest in obtaining, as soon as possible during the enlargement process, a clear accession timeframe. The prospects of joining the EU were expected to have a positive effect on the level of confidence of the international financial institutions, rating agencies and foreign investors. This became a reality in relation to the IMF, World Bank and prestigious rating agencies which reacted favourably after the clarification of the timetable for Romania's accession. Another example, such as the proliferation, lately, of investments by leading supermarket chains could also represent empirical evidence that the signing of the Accession Treaty in April 2005 is associated with higher investor expectations.

High economic growth rates have been a common denominator of the 10 CEE countries in the last few years. Although economic growth depends on a number of interdependent factors, not least the policies pursued by governments, the prospect of membership is generally accepted as having contributed to these high rates. As far as Romania is concerned, starting from late 1999, it witnessed steady GDP growth rates, among the highest in the region, with an increase of 8.3% in 2004 and one estimated at 5.5%-6.0% for 2005.

Among the benefits already incurred or expected as a consequence of EU membership, one could mention: an increase in the competitiveness of domestic products, as a result of the pressure of the single market and higher EU standards; productivity gains and technology transfers, as well as increased

[1]   Romania is currently receiving around €1 billion *per annum* in pre-accession aid. Financial transfers will almost double after accession

specialization in certain industries and areas where tradition, skills and other comparative advantages exist; a higher level of consumer protection; better environmental protection; a new dynamic in the capital markets, with beneficial effects throughout the economy; and improved access to the internal market (especially for the sensitive areas of agriculture and labour).

Although the potential for financial transfers (through the Structural Funds or the Common Agricultural Policy) was not originally a central motivation for EU membership, as the date of accession draws nearer and as the costs of membership also become clearer, net financial benefits have definitely occupied a more prominent place in pro-EU arguments domestically. Expectations are that access to structural funds will contribute to a more balanced development of the regions, sustainable rural development, as well as infrastructure development (mainly transport infrastructure, which is a priority in Romania). As a future member with a relatively large agricultural sector, accession will bring Romania benefits such as increased productivity, improved access to EU markets and an increase in farmers' income. The case of the Polish farmers, a group initially opposed to EU accession, but which has become significantly better off since membership, is an example often cited in favour of membership.

Of course there will not be only winners; there will certainly be companies which will not survive the competitive pressures and restructuring and technological improvement in some sectors is essential for survival. Preparing for accession already brings a more effective enforcement of the EU's strict rules on competition, public procurement, the movement of capital, intellectual property rights, etc. This will lead to a healthier economic environment, with increased efficiency and competitiveness, but will also act on the market like a process of natural selection, eliminating the weak and consolidating the viable operators.

In the international arena, given the weight and influence of the EU, the new member states rightly perceive that their economic and trade interests will be better protected in bodies such as the WTO, the OECD, and the World Intellectual Property Organization. On the other hand, the new challenge will lie in the individual ability to filter into the common EU position particular national interests on a given issue.

But perhaps the main effect of the prospect of EU membership has been its role as an anchor of the reform process. The drive to join the EU has been one of the most powerful incentives for undertaking major reforms in all candidate countries. Through the annual reports of the European Commission, the EU has ensured constant and consistent external pressure, helping to ensure the continuity of reform efforts. The role of anchor for the reform process offered by the credible prospect of membership has been reinforced by tangible benefits resulting from conditional access to pre accession aid, freer trade and political support. The entire multidimensional process of preparing for EU accession has thus acted as a catalyst and facilitator of reforms and for the modernization of society as a whole.

In this context, besides the political or economic interests linked to EU accession, one could state without hesitation that a fundamental interest of any candidate country is to benefit, in its efforts towards modernisation, from the impressive transformative power of the EU. The desire for and the prospect of EU membership have had the most profound and unique, though sometimes difficult to quantify, effect on every dimension of society in applicant countries, be it the working of the administration, the rebuilding of civil society, relations between the main political actors, or among the institutions of the state, or inter-ethnic relations.

EU accession proper will also represent the pinnacle of the transformation of the way we, as new members, perceive ourselves and of the way we relate to our European partners. In a sense, it will represent the moment when the journey towards 'we and they' becoming 'us' will have reached its destination. One of the reasons behind the observer status period in the various EU institutions, between the signing of the Accession Treaty and actual accession, is the smooth transition from the 'EU-candidate' two-player game to the 'EU-27' multi-player game. It will imply, first of all, a radical change in mentality when dealing with EU affairs. We will no longer be talking to and negotiating with the 'EU side', but we will be full participants in the work of the EU institutions representing the governments of the member states and their citizens. As a member, we will have to define and defend our interests in relation to the issues on the table, be aware of the importance and the limitations of our individual voice and fully accept the decisions taken in common.

On the international scene, the new member states will gain in status in at least two ways. As participants in the Common Foreign and Security Policy, they will have a direct say in and contribution to the external policies of one the main global players. Also, as member of the EU, individual status and implicit influence vis-à-vis third countries will certainly grow. One can also assume that the foreign policy priorities of a new member state can occupy a place among the EU's priorities, especially if common interests are at stake, such as, for example, those related to neighbouring areas.

As concerns the current perceptions and expectations of the Romanian citizen, the findings of a 2005 Eurobarometer poll are very relevant.[2] Among the

---

[2] European Commission, *Eurobarometer* 62, Brussels, May 2005. The survey was conducted in autumn 2004 and is available at http://europa.eu.int/comm/public_opinion/archives/eb/eb62/eb62_en.htm.

member and acceding states, Romania is the country with the highest degree of trust in EU institutions (74%). This is second only to the Church (82%). Even if knowledge about EU issues is relatively low statistically the respondents with higher levels of information are the ones most supportive of the integration process. Regarding individual perceptions about membership, the EU is frequently associated with freedom of travel and work (64%), while economic prosperity and peace are cited in second place. On the negative side, EU membership is associated with concerns relating to unemployment and price increases. Romanians' expectations with regard to the EU's role in solving problems are also very high. Most of them expect the EU to play an active and positive role in dealing with issues such as fighting terrorism (70%), foreign affairs (64%), the economic situation (64%), combating crime (62%), environmental protection (61%), healthcare and education (50%). The prospects of EU accession can be considered as contributing significantly to an optimistic view about the future, with 62% of the Romanians believing that their life will improve in the next five years. Young people represent the population category with the highest trust in the integration of Romania in the EU and also the most optimistic (78% believe life will improve in the next 5 years).

SOME CONCLUSIONS

The initial debate in Romania on EU membership, to the extent that there was one, was concerned with joining the EU as a matter of principle, rather than with the implications of membership for specific policies or interest groups. The very high degree of consensus among political actors and analysts and public opinion have contributed to the consistency of domestic policy on accession to the EU throughout the last decade,[3] although a variable pace in implementing internal reforms has, sometimes, led to ups and downs in the speed with which the country has advanced towards meeting EU requirements.

Apart from the historical, cultural and emotional motivations, EU integration has also been a strategic option for Romania. It was seen as being the only viable option, offering the appropriate framework for dealing with the current and future challenges on the international scene. Given the EU's size and economic influence, membership was seen as a much better way of facing the challenges of globalization than the traditional political and economic system limited to the national borders. The EU is a living organism, in continuous transformation, the result of internal as well as external factors, including

---

[3] Relevant in this respect is the fact that the Accession Treaty received the unanimous endorsement of the Romanian Parliament on 17 May 2005.

successive enlargements. Romania's interest is to accede to an EU that will continue to function according to the same principles that have guided its existence since the beginning: an EU based on economic performance combined with economic, social and territorial cohesion; an EU that is not too distant from its citizens; and an EU preserving the different national specificities which make up its cultural richness and diversity. The Constitutional Treaty, whose entry into force is clearly in doubt, offers new prospects for Europe to prepare itself better for the challenges and opportunities at the beginning of this century, while preserving the principles on which the process of European integration has been based. Throughout the process, Romania has been present, as observer, to the drafting of the Treaty and has been looking forward to joining in 2007 an EU defined by this new legal foundation. As this now seems impossible, the accession of Romania and Bulgaria to the EU will mark, instead of a new beginning under a new Treaty, the completion of the journey designed at Nice in 2000 when the institutional decisions for an EU of 27 were taken. It will represent the natural conclusion of the fifth EU enlargement process, as well as the fulfilment of Romania's main policy objective of the last decade.

CHAPTER NINE

Romania and the Future of the European Union

Adrian Severin

Soon Romania is likely to become a member of the European Union (EU). Within such a context it is important to determine what Romania is going to bring to the EU and how it will behave once inside. Membership will become effective at a time when the EU needs dramatic internal changes and faces an historic crisis. What will be the attitude of Romania with respect to such challenges? What are its options concerning the transformation of the EU? How and in what direction could Romanian membership influence the development of the EU? The opinion of today's political elite and the present inclinations of the public are less relevant. What is really important are the essential characteristics of the way in which Romanians solve universal problems and define their national interest within a European perspective. Starting from Romanian identity – both in cultural and in geopolitical terms – this chapter seeks to provide answers.

ROMANIA AND THE EU: ANTHROPOLOGICAL AND GEOPOLITICAL BACKGROUND

Romanians believe that the futures of the EU and Romania are inextricably linked. There is a synchrony between them. One of the most well-known and respected slogans in Romanian history is 'the union makes the power!'. Guided by this slogan the Romanian Principalities united in 1859 and Greater Romania was formed in 1918. The sense of unity explains the great popular support of Romanians not only for Romania's involvement in European integration, but also for the development of the EU as a more federal entity.

The view that 'unity is a necessity' is inspired by the anthropological background of the Romanian family – characterized by egalitarianism and authority – and by the history of the Romanians who have had to survive in the neighbourhood of several rival empires.

Egalitarianism

The traditional organization of the Romanian family is based on the relationship between parents and children, on the one hand, and between brothers, on the other. This has been transferred into their Orthodox religion (expressing the concept of the ideal city in heaven) and into the ideas that form the basis of their concept of the ideal city on earth. It also explains not only their particular outlook, but also their rejection of ethnocentric nationalism. As with almost all Latin peoples in Europe, for Romanians human beings are equal and the citizen is just an expression of the universal person. Thus lacking an organic view on the concept of nation, Romanians attach to the concept of nation a geopolitical as opposed to cultural connotation. This has led to an instinctive tolerance which is indifferent to culture and identity-based diversity. Therefore, even if very conservative, Romanian society is not obsessed by the past and it is not looking for temporal continuity and the persistence of the past in the present and its transmission into the future. Consequently, Romanians are not affected by that kind of national egoism which today hampers the progress of the EU towards a more federal system. On the contrary, their universalistic approach – which is the other face of their individualism – encourages thoughts of and support for a political Europe.

There is nothing in the self-perception and identity of Romanians that is resistant to the deepening of European integration. If the future of Europe depends on the capacity of Europeans to define 'the other' or 'the alien' or 'the stranger', Romanians, by virtue of their capacity to accept and integrate the stranger, raise no objections. On the contrary they are among its greatest supporters.

At the same time, Romanian conservatism, unconstrained as it is by the past, could be described as a 'progressive conservatism'. It is about the speed of change and not a refusal to change. Romanians are always modernizing but they do it at a very slow pace. They readily accept new forms but they will fill those forms with new substance much later. Consequently the EU should not expect from Romania a push for rapid internal transformation. Equally, it should not fear Romanian opposition to modernization or to any measure aimed at increasing Europe's capacity to cope better with the opportunities, dangers and challenges of the contemporary multi-polar and globalized world.

Authority

Romanians possess a readiness to accept and a desire to benefit from hierarchical order. Romanians are definitely looking for protection from above. If the EU can protect them better or add something to the protection they already receive from the Romanian state, the more attractive it is. From this perspective, we can predict that while welcoming the action and the intervention of the EU, Romanians as members will seek enhancement of the principles underpinning 'social Europe'. For Romanians, Europe is needed more in order to ensure solidarity than it is to arbitrate free competition. Economic, social and territorial cohesion and EU policies leading to them are and will be of a paramount importance for Romanians. Likewise, any action meant to promote social inclusion will be more important in the eyes of Romanians than those promoting equality of opportunity.

Romanians are not like the British, the Dutch and the Danes who, due to their liberalism, are more inclined to the free market and free competition, thus accepting inequality. Equally, Romanians are unlike the Germans, the Austrians and the Swedes with their tendency to emphasise the role of the state in making accepted inequality decently bearable and ascribing it the role of a catalyst for competition and progress. Instead, Romanians call on public authorities to respect and to ensure equality among individuals. This seemingly schizophrenic combination of authority and equality places obvious limits on authority. Thus for Romanians authority is always relative and it is more accepted rather than desired. Romanians are used to bargain with authority rather than to respect it. As far as the role of authority is concerned, Romanians, because of their egalitarian inclinations, find themselves somewhere between British liberalism and the German preference for state-inspired order. Consequently, Romanians will share Anglo-Saxon Europe's commitment to – it is true, for different reasons – the principle and the mechanisms of subsidiarity. However, Romanians' support for the principle of subsidiarity is not as strong as to lead them to insist on an increasing role for national parliaments within the EU's decision-making processes.

This all suggests that Romanians are ready for an EU that is more federal – in the continental European sense – provided that such a Union does not disrupt the geopolitical equilibrium which has been achieved within the borders of the nation-state. In other words, the Romanian mood will naturally be in favour of a European federation of nation-states.

Historical Experience and Historical Accidents

For modern Romania's political outlook the most influential external phenomena have been Russian expansionism and Hungarian ethno-nationalism. National unity was the most obvious response to them; a national unity for geopolitical and not for ethnic reasons. Of these two threats, the Russian one has long been the bigger and has obliged Romania to look westwards. Since its immediate western neighbour used to be the Austro-Hungarian Empire the only realistic choice was the European 'Far West'. Hence due to cultural, historical and political affinities with the three big Western countries – Germany, France and Britain – closer links were established, notably with the first two. Later they would become the engines of European integration.

As for Hungary, being much smaller and between Romania and the European 'Far West', a traditional strategy of confrontation was replaced relatively soon after the end of the Cold War, namely in 1997, by a strategy of partnership. The basic principle for Romanian foreign policy is therefore to be always in the same alliance with Hungary and to avoid being caught in the middle between Russia and a divided Euro-Atlantic space or between Russia and the European Occident (especially the Central European powers). The need for a strong EU as a counterweight to Russia is a key rule. Such a strong EU means a prosperous free market and a vibrant economy only to the extent that economic strength is the basis for real power. For controlling and using economic resources in a meaningful way one needs a political Europe. Therefore, for Romania the EU is and remains first and foremost a political project, albeit one to be achieved via economic means. Thus the Romanian vision for the future of the EU is extremely close to the vision of the founding fathers of European integration.

While being fully European and fully committed to Europe, Romania is a country with a Euro-Atlantic vocation. Three factors account for this. First, Romania finds itself located at the crossroad of the interests of major global actors (the EU, the United States, Russia and even China). Second, Romania is located in some very strategic global communication corridors that connect it with the Atlantic – via the Danube, Main and Rhine rivers – and through the Black Sea with the Mediterranean Sea and – further through the Caucasus – the Caspian Sea. Third, Romania has paid one of the largest prices for intra-European fighting in the two World Wars of the Twentieth Century. Romania therefore understands the crucial role of the United States in maintaining the equilibrium between the European powers and at the same time in ensuring European security against global threats. In the light of the lessons learnt from history, Romania resists any understanding between Russia and Western Europeans that ignores or excludes the Anglo-American factor from the geopolitical future of Europe.

As a consequence Romania will act within the EU for a common European foreign, security and defence policy. This implies the establishment of a European defence identity and of a European capacity to develop its own military technologies. Romania will, however, speak against a decoupling of Europe from NATO's collective defence system. From Romania's point of view the strengthening of the EU's military capabilities should not undermine but rather facilitate transatlantic cooperation by creating opportunities for fairer burden sharing.

As a soon to be border member of the EU Romania understands that any confrontation with or within the EU's neighbourhood affects it as one of the weakest, most exposed and most vulnerable member states. Therefore, Romania has a vital interest in a friendly, democratic, stable and prosperous neighbourhood for the EU. At the same time and for similar reasons one can expect that Romania will support Turkey's accession to the EU as well as that of Moldova, Ukraine, Belarus and of the Western Balkan countries. Accession will, of course, only be acceptable if these countries meet the appropriate criteria. The geopolitical equilibrium in the Balkan region – which will require the reintegration of Serbia in the South Danube security system – and the consolidation of the EU presence in the Black Sea region are priorities of particular strategic interest for Romania. At the same time, once achieved, they will increase the EU's standing as a global actor. There is no contradiction between these priorities and the EU's own aspirations.

ROMANIA IN THE EU

What will motivate Romanians to show loyalty towards the EU and its institutions? Undoubtedly it will not be a common language or common cultural traditions. There are nevertheless factors that will motivate loyalty. These, according to opinion poll and other research data, are encapsulated in a single concept with four dimensions. The concept is 'security' and the four dimensions are individual/personal security, collective/social security, cultural/national security and global/international security. These are common to all Europeans. They cover peoples' expectations of prosperity, hard security, freedom and dignity. If the EU is unable to enhance such security, integration as a political project will fail.

With regard to *individual security* Romania has previously expressed its support for a common area of freedom, security and justice and for the merger of the EU's third pillar with the other two. Within this context it has presented a vision which combines the Charter of Fundamental Rights – which should become legally binding and should establish basic political, social and economic freedoms and rights – with European citizenship and with a

European judicial system which would allow the individual right of recourse to the European Courts once national procedures have been exhausted. As a member of the Council of Europe, Romania proposed either merger of the European Court of Human Rights with the European Court of Justice or providing access for the EU to the European Convention on Human Rights. Both would have avoided conflicts between European jurisdictions, norms and standards as well as an *a la carte* approach to human rights. Likewise, the automatic recognition of judicial sentences in one EU member state by the authorities of all other member states was suggested. Romania also expressed the need both to strengthen Europol and to transfer more policing competences to the EU level (at least where trans-border crimes are concerned) and to create a European Prosecutor's Office (at least for fiscal fraud). Romania has also spoken in favour of a single European border police, by necessity accompanied by a joint financing instrument.

With regard to *social security* Romania has expressed the opinion that without a 'social Europe' the future of the EU is uncertain. From this perspective it has been proposed that national economic and social policies should be harmonized and become subject to a degree of coordination on a federal basis. 'Structural intervention is absolutely necessary for the preservation of economic and social cohesion in an enlarged Europe, where the member states stick to the same parameters and the same economic policies. The aspect concerning redistribution under the conditions of an Economic and Monetary Union is vital, as it is the principle of European solidarity to remain at the origin of these policies.' So wrote the former Romanian Prime Minister, Adrian Năstase in 2001. Along these lines Romanian participants in the European Convention proposed or supported the idea of a European Minister for the Economy and Development or a European Minister for Financial and Social Affairs, both being vice-presidents of the European Commission. They also spoke in favour of the harmonization, at least partial, of tax policies, for the extension of the open method of coordination and for easier recourse to enhanced cooperation. Romanian members of the European Convention stressed the unique character of the 2004 enlargement of the EU and of the internal transformations linked to it and drew attention to the unprecedented economic and social disparities it will bring to the EU. The main principle supported by Romanian participants was that the internal market and monetary union could not function – or at least could not function to the full satisfaction of European citizens – without a common economic and tax policy. This is vital for a common social policy, which must be integrated together with the other internal policies into a general policy framework, which must be supported by common external action, which has as its ultimate form a common defence policy.

As for *national security* Romanians look to a future in a new European society comprising a multitude of cultures. In preparation for this future Romania has transformed itself from an ethnic state – as it was when the nation-state was born – into a civic and multicultural state. At the same time Romania expects that within an EU of 'national minorities' two simultaneous processes will take place. On the one hand the asymmetrical relationship between national majority and national minorities will be replaced by a new symmetrical relationship between 'national communities' based on a system of global subsidiarity. This will eliminate the natural frustrations of the minorities and the unavoidable tensions characterizing asymmetrical relationships, both of which are sources of insecurity. On the other hand, the blurring of nation-states' borders will facilitate a de-dramatized reconstitution of old cultural nations, decoupling at the same time cultural rights from territorial rights. Thus Europe's existing multidimensional socio-cultural tissue will be given a new lease of life as geopolitical fears related to territorial claims for ethnic reasons become groundless. Consequently within the European Convention the Romanian representatives called for a communitarization of the standards and protection of cultural-national rights as a means to guarantee cultural diversity and avoid the use by national communities of legitimate aspirations for achieving geopolitical goals.

International security raises the problem of the EU's own geopolitical identity. In an era of globalization, territorial contiguity and inter-regional cooperation are of a paramount importance. The EU itself recognized this as much when it decided to develop a dedicated neighbourhood policy. The focus on its neighbourhood reflects the EU's geopolitical ambitions and responsibilities. An EU contiguous with the Black Sea region is different from a geopolitical identity point of view to an EU stretching only as far as the mid-course of the Danube. At the same time, its transition from market to power depends very much on the opportunities the EU has to assume more responsibility internationally.

Romania will be important for the EU as a market. It could also be important as a political agent able to support and promote the EU's regional and sub-regional strategies. Four regions should be noted, namely: Central Europe, to which Romania culturally and geopolitically belongs and where it is in a position to develop a cooperative security architecture based on variable geometry; Eastern Europe, where a neighbourhood comprising Ukraine, Moldova and Russia has always required a strong Romania in order that the region be less problematic for Western Europe; South-Eastern Europe (the Balkans), where Romania has a tradition of intense contacts unburdened by hatred and conflict; and the Black Sea region (Transcaucasia included) which is crossed by many strategic transportation corridors whose security must be protected. In all these regions Romania has the capacity to play a pivotal role in sub-regional cooperation arrangements. These could either be integrated as elements of a pan-European security structure or exist merely as a friendly neighbourhood for a United Europe. Against this background, Romanian representatives within the European Convention supported the establishment of a European Union Foreign Minister as well as the extension of qualified majority voting to decisions on the EU's external action.

ROMANIA AND THE EUROPEAN CONSTITUTION

According to public opinion polls Romanians are very enthusiastic about European integration. They support whole-heartedly not only Romania's integration into the EU but also the deepening of the Union. For Romanians it is obvious too that the EU is today confronted with various challenges posed by globalization. In fact, it is globalization which makes both the enlargement and the deepening of the EU a necessity.

Indeed, enlargement is not simply compensation offered to the Central and Eastern European countries allegedly abandoned at the end of World War II behind the Iron Curtain and placed at the mercy of Soviet totalitarianism. It is not a sense of moral duty that explains the decision of the EU to open its doors to new members. Enlargement is taking place due to the need to reconcile Europe's history and geography. Without such a reconciliation the EU could not take advantage of Europe's human and natural resources; could not provide itself with the opportunity to become more coherent and to create pan-European economic, social and territorial cohesion. It could not face the competition from other centres in our multi-polar globalized world. It could not overcome its demographic problems and cope with its structural weaknesses. Nor could it obtain the recognition of its rights and status as a global player. On the other hand the deepening of the EU should not be regarded only as the consequence of the enlargement process. An EU with more members certainly needs political institutions able to better harmonize and coordinate national agendas, options and actions, as well as decision-making procedures able to create reasonable majorities which generate legitimacy for action. But deepening is necessary irrespective of enlargement. Globalization and competition require a more efficient management of the EU member states' common interests. For this the transformation of the EU as a market into a political Europe is indispensable. Enlargement depends on how the EU defines its identity in a globalized world and it will also reflect that definition. This ideally combines the objective characteristics of Europe's geography and history, and the present aspirations of its peoples.

Starting from such convictions, Romania's representatives in the European Convention supported the principle of the dual nature and the dual legitimacy of the EU as a union of states and a union of citizens. Hence Romania has accepted the principle of the double majority (states and people) in EU decision-making. Likewise, it has expressed the opinion that the roles of the Commission – the size of which should be determined by the need of efficiency and not the principle of 'one state, one commissioner' – and of the European Parliament should be increased in order to give them the capacity to address effectively common European interests. Within this context the principle of 'fewer competences but their more federal exercise' was expressed.

As a member, Romania is going to be the biggest among the small and the smallest among the big EU member states. Romania is keenly interested in the efficiency more than in the representativeness of the EU's institutions. Consequently it understands that the adoption of decisions by unanimity – which ultimately means each member state has a veto – is neither an effective nor a feasible way forward for the weaker members. For them, apparent equality in law is outweighed by the inequality in political and economic potential. Likewise Romania understands that one needs majorities that can decide rather than minorities which can block a decision. Vetoes can prevent decisions but cannot solve problems. Therefore Romania is likely to be in favour of the extension of QMV to all decisions which do not concern the transfer of competences either from the member states to the EU or vice versa.

Many Romanians favoured a pan-European referendum as opposed to national votes on the European Constitutional Treaty. This could have taken place after all national parliaments had ratified the document on the same day in all member states with the outcome being determined by a pan-European and not a majority in each of the member states. In the light of current difficulties in ratifying the Constitutional Treaty, Romania, once in the EU, will push for a new impetus to this integration process. This will very much be consistent with the Romanian opinion that the current transformation of the EU is not a mere reform but the re-founding of the Union. Within this context Romania definitely sees itself as a co-founding state of a new political Europe, a new transborder European democracy. It will most probably behave as such too.

CONCLUSION

Romania needs the EU as much as the EU needs Romania. Romanians have already defined their strategic interests within a European framework admitting that what is good for Europe is also good for Romania. They will certainly work in order to prove that the opposite is also true: what is good for Romania is good for Europe. In this respect they will try to synthesise Romania's European priorities with the EU's priorities in Romania. Within this framework a political EU built as a transnational pan-European democracy will be the goal and the priority of Romania as a new member. Since this will require a virtual re-foundation of the EU, Romania will act and perceive itself as a new founding member of a new EU.

CHAPTER TEN

Romania and the Challenges of the Internal Market

Dragoș Negrescu

Depending on the quarters from which it is looked at, Romania's imminent accession to the European Union (EU) raises two categories of fears. Externally, concerns are expressed about the risk of having the 'four freedoms' abused by a competitor unable to play by the rules. Domestically, an abrupt change of mood has been noticeable since the end of 2004, when official statements exclusively emphasizing the advantages of accession have given way to a pseudo-realism embodied in a continuous lamenting of the consequences of the 'integration shock'. There are precious few concrete arguments brought in favour of either of the two theses, but this is not regarded as an impediment by the proponents of the 'domesday scenario'.

This chapter does not attempt to offer a formal and comprehensive rebuttal of these fears, not only because a thorough quantitative analysis is beyond its scope, but also because the concerns themselves are long on drama and short of substance. It nonetheless challenges the received wisdom of a 'clash of civilizations' on Day One of Romania's EU membership. The main assumption around which these arguments are centred, and which is largely neglected by most commentators, is that a good deal of the adjustment of the Romanian economy to the rigours of the Internal Market has already taken place.

There are two main reasons why this is the case: the obligations deriving from Romania's Europe Agreement; and the process of accession negotiations carried out since 2000. Both have induced an internalization by Romania of a good deal of Internal Market rules well ahead of accession, thus greatly minimizing the size of the much feared 'accession shock'. Of course, the preparation of Romania is not complete and can vary quite significantly from one area of the Internal Market to another. Accordingly, wherever preparation is well advanced, accession will bring no changes, while the actual shocks will concern only those areas where preparation is lagging behind. In order to explore this *problématique* in a systematic way, the chapter follows broadly the content of the negotiation chapters.

FREE MOVEMENT OF GOODS

The Europe Agreement committed Romania to free trade in industrial goods with the EU. This has been fully realized – as far as overt restrictions (tariffs and quotas) are concerned – since the beginning of 2002.

The bilateral trade regime in *agricultural goods*, however, is different. Originally, only limited bilateral concessions were negotiated on a case-by-case basis, but four other rounds of market opening negotiations have followed, so that a good deal of the respective agricultural markets of the two parties are now open for reciprocal exports. Granted, free trade does not yet exist, so further reductions of trade barriers will have to occur upon accession, but it is unlikely that they will bring about dramatic changes to Romanian agriculture. The latter is already confronted with significant import competition from EU producers and accession carries with it two important counterweights: access to Common Agricultural Policy (CAP) subsidies and larger export market outlets (because full liberalization will be symmetrical). Generally speaking, the fate of Romania's agriculture has no particular reason to worsen post-accession. Ironically, its most often invoked weakness – the fact that a significant proportion of agricultural exploitations are too small, hence uncompetitive and oriented towards self-consumption – becomes a protective feature in the context of accession. Indeed, farmers who are de-coupled from the market have nothing to fear from market developments triggered by accession. This is not to say that the state of and perspectives for Romanian agriculture are rosy, but this sector is certainly not going to be the sacrificial lamb of Romania's EU membership. If anything, the gradual inclusion of Romania's agricultural sector in the mechanisms of the CAP should facilitate the process of phasing out inefficient smallholdings because the market value of land should increase, thus making it more attractive for current farmers to quit and hence facilitate consolidation.

Turning back to *industrial products*, it should be noted that total fulfilment by Romania of its commitments has involved a rather long learning curve. It is interesting to follow how, gradually, the approach of GATT and then the World Trade Organization (WTO), centred on border restrictions and national treatment as far as domestic measures are concerned, was superseded by the

'EU approach', whereby restrictions to intra-EU trade are prohibited irrespective of whether the same treatment is applied to domestically-produced goods. In a first stage (until 1997), also taking advantage of transitional periods provided by the Europe Agreement, Romania applied overt quantitative restrictions (quotas and even outright bans) on several categories of exports, notably hides and skins, raw and summarily processed wood, and ferrous and non-ferrous scrap. The reason behind these measures was obvious and admitted as such by the authorities: ensuring access to cheap raw materials for the local processors of the said goods, thanks to the wedge driven between their domestic and international prices, respectively, by the restrictions.

Ensuing (until 2000) was a period during which various measures of equivalent effect to quantitative restrictions were used: export licences for scrap were only issued to applicants proving that they supplied equivalent quantities on the domestic market; and discriminatory indirect taxes were imposed on imported spirits and, especially, cigarettes. Finally, in 2001–2002 a comprehensive effort was made to 'package' trade restrictions as legitimate measures meant to protect the environment and consumers. Hence, raw wood exports were prohibited; special environment fees were levied and cumbersome VAT refund procedures imposed on wood and scrap exports; a licensing regime for selected second-hand goods (clothes, tyres, consumer durables) entailed more demanding requirements for imports; and longer transition periods for the implementation of 'Euro 3' car exhaust norms were granted for domestically-produced vehicles.

It is only since the beginning of 2003 that full compatibility with free trade 'WTO-style' could be ensured between Romania and the EU for industrial goods. Moving further, to free trade 'EU-style' is more demanding. Romania nonetheless made an important step forward starting with 2004 when a substantial streamlining of the coverage of automatic licences was undertaken: the number of (8-digit) tariff positions so covered was reduced from 181 to just 95. Various goods – such as non-ferrous ores and scrap, raw hides, raw and summarily processed wood, and ferrous scrap – are still subject to this regime. The whole system is to be abolished on accession to the EU. This will leave in place one single instrument which, based on the jurisprudence of the European Court of Justice (ECJ), should be qualified as a 'measure having equivalent effect': price controls applied to various goods and services, and to imported medicines for human use in particular. Unless this problem (which has existed for over 4 years) is solved soon, it may well become the first case brought against Romania at the ECJ.

Technical barriers to trade. Accession to the EU should make no difference to Romanian exports as far as product standards and technical regulations are concerned. Indeed, since about 70% of the country's exports already go to the European market, and taking also into account the worldwide recognition of many European standards, it is certain that practically all Romanian exports are already compliant with these norms. Also, since they have already been accepted on the European market, the conformity assessment issue has also been solved.

Three issues should be noted, however. The first concerns the enforcement of production process norms. These will affect mainly the production of liquid fuels and some chemicals. While official estimates place the 'price tag' of internalizing the environment *acquis* at €29 billion, this figure also includes the costs of complying with environment norms not directly related to production processes, such as waste management and air quality. Besides, this estimate covers the cost of rendering environment-compliant all existing production facilities, thus implying that all of them should be kept in operation, while there might well be compelling economic justifications for simply closing down some of them.

Second there is a risk that the mutual recognition principle will be exploited for the purpose of placing on the European market goods belonging to the 'non-harmonised' categories which do not comply with the 'mandatory require-ments' relating to the protection of public health and the consumer. Since the mutual recognition principle does not establish an absolute presumption of equivalence of the objectives of national regulations, but only a rebuttable one, this risk can be safely discounted. Moreover, it would hardly make any commercial sense for the vast majority of Romanian producers already present on the European market to come up with goods not known to the consumer.

A third issues concerns difficulties in complying with technical requirements in the 'harmonized' sectors. The risk here is minimized by the fact that, according to the Romanian standardization institution (ASRO), over 99% of the standards adopted by CEN and CENELEC had been transposed as of the end of 2004, a performance which – if confirmed – would dwarf that of several existing EU member states. However, the sheer transposition of European norms and standards is not sufficient unless accompanied by an effective market surveillance system, which is not exactly a strong point in Romania. This notwithstanding, the risk that actual compliance with the relevant *acquis* is not satisfactory only arises if there is widespread segregation – in the 'harmonized sectors' – between production for the domestic market and production for export where proof of compliance with the European norms is a must. Since no compelling indications in this sense exist, one may safely discount this risk as well.

Summing up, the long period during which Romania was only a passive actor in the area of product norms and standards has the positive side effect that a very high degree of compatibility with European norms and standards was already achieved. This makes it counterproductive to revert to national norms and standards in the non-harmonised area after accession and ensures substantial compliance in the harmonized area.

Public procurement is one of the few areas where the Europe Agreement has exerted only minimal influence. Although Romanian companies have enjoyed over the last decade complete and non-discriminatory access to the public procurement procedures carried out in EU member states, this has not been reflected in any significant business gains. Obviously, nothing changes in this respect with accession. Conversely, access of EU companies to the Romanian public procurement market has long been affected by various discriminatory restrictions: provisions reserving the award of certain contracts to local suppliers only (until 2001) and preferential margins granted to local bidders (until the end of 2004). Paradoxically, it is not these departures from the national treatment regime that constitute the worst aspect of the Romanian public procurement system, but rather the way this system worked irrespective of the origin of the bidders. Whereas, since 2001 the legal framework was, by and large, in line with the relevant EU directives, the actual implementation of the rules was nothing short of catastrophic. Succinctly put, the vast majority of Romanian public procurement was carried out in extreme ways. Either competitive bidding was systematically by-passed and direct attribution was used (the much publicized BECHTEL and EADS cases were only the tip of the iceberg) or a blunt system of so-called *e-procurement*, in force since 2002, and denying civil servants any discretion was used.

Consequently, the rationing of access to the top-tier of Romanian public procurement was not done according to the nationality of the bidders, but rather based on their willingness to engage in questionable tactics (including, sometimes, the mobilisation of their home country embassy). As concerns the e-procurement system, which is completely unsuitable for the procurement of anything other than simple goods, its failure – due to its rigidity – to deliver decent outcomes in several important cases (most recently, the construction of several hundred defective sporting halls) demonstrates that there is no miracle solution to the problem of poor administrative capacity and one needs reasonably competent and honest administrators rather than human appendices to computers.

Indisputably, a good system of redress procedures would have been far more useful than the ill-thought-out e-procurement experiment. Since it implies the assertion of jurisdictional prerogatives by the ECJ, the influence of accession in this area may be dramatic. Moreover, it can only have positive effects: better value for money will be obtained at no particular cost to domestic production because, as mentioned earlier, since 2001 nationality has not been the prominent award criteria.

FREE MOVEMENT OF SERVICES

For the sake of simplicity, this vast area is broken down according to the 'modes of supply' described in the General Agreement on Trade in Services, though in a different order than that featuring in the said text.

First, regarding the consumption of services by residents on the territory of another country, there is strictly nothing new that accession should entail. Second, there is supply through commercial presence in the territory of another country. Here the Europe Agreement contained rather strong commitments, albeit asymmetric ones in the sense that the obligations of the EU are more comprehensive in terms of sectors covered. Romania retained the right to deny the free exercise of the right of establishment in several areas, including in particular legal services, real estate, gambling and lotteries. However, a long list of laws has been enacted over the years which introduced restrictions of access in other sectors, such as inland waterways transport and security services. All these limitations should disappear by the date of accession at the latest, though it is difficult to understand why the EU has accepted such a deadline in connection with sectors where Romania has a contractual obligation to grant the right of establishment to EU companies.

Third, there is the matter of supply through the presence of natural persons in the territory of another country. To a large extent, this has been tackled in the context of the negotiations on the free movement of persons. The list of professions where citizenship is a requirement for their exercise in Romania is impressive: doctors, lawyers, architects, to name but a few. As in the case described above, no such restrictions will be allowed to stay in place after accession. Having said that, the net static effect of the reciprocal liberalization of this mode of supply should not be detrimental to Romania given that far more of its nationals are likely to make use of the right to exercise their professions in other EU member states than vice versa. However, in a dynamic perspective it is not entirely inappropriate to express concerns about the likelihood of a *brain drain* and its negative consequences on Romania, especially as long as the state continues to offer higher education for free to a large number of students.

Finally, there is supply from the territory of one country into the territory of another country. This mode of supply is only slowly being liberalized even among existing member states. And there is much resistance as the recent attempt to move things forward, via the controversial Bolkestein Directive has proved. As the cross-border delivery of services is hampered by various determinants (among which cultural ones are prominent) the EU market continues to be segmented along national lines. Nevertheless, while no dramatic developments will occur with this mode of supply once Romania joins the EU there are important positive spillover effects to be expected, mainly as a result of implementing the financial services *acquis*. Thanks to a combination of strict prudential requirements and strong supervisory capabilities, this *acquis* shapes a sound financial sector which is the inescapable determinant of a dynamic real economy. The degree of internalization of the financial services *acquis* in Romania is very uneven, with banking being the clear leader and insurance the unchallenged laggard. The silver-lining is that this ranking accurately reflects the degree of development of each of these areas in Romania, so that the economic impact of something going wrong in one sub-system, weighted by the likelihood of this happening, is probably comparable across all three sub-systems: banking, securities, and insurance.

FREE MOVEMENT OF CAPITAL

Although it covers several other topics (right of establishment, acquisition by EU citizens of land, and 'golden shares'), the crucial component of the free movement of capital chapter relates to the elimination of all restrictions to the movement of capital flows inside and outside the country. The Europe Agreement imposed obligations only in respect of those capital flows recorded in the current account, being silent as concerns the other side of the balance of payments. However, this does not mean that capital account liberalization may be achieved in one fell swoop, as of the date of accession. Consequently, the National Bank of Romania (NBR) produced in 2001 a cautious plan for the gradual liberalisation of capital movements. This was built around notions that long-term movements should be deregulated before short-term ones and inflows should be freed before the corresponding outflows. So far, the plan has been implemented as envisaged with the notable exception of the liberalization of access of non-residents to deposit accounts denominated in the national currency, where the deadline was put off by 14 months, until April 2005. The remaining categories of flows (operations with securities routinely traded on the money market) are due to be liberalised only upon accession.

The liberalization of capital movements has stirred concerns and some influential Romanian economists have waged a long battle trying to persuade NBR to postpone further the liberalization move undertaken in the spring of 2005 until 'the conditions are ripe'. Many of their reservations, though copiously inspired from the East Asian debacle of 1997–98, are understandable. However, the one thing they failed to explain is how a *sine die* postponement of the liberalization is consonant with a *fixed date* accession to the EU. Besides, they seem not to place enough faith in the 'antibodies' that accession carries with it and which are able to avert a repetition of the East Asian syndrome: a sound financial sector, given compliance with the demanding requirements of the financial services *acquis*; and an increase of credibility which goes *pari passu* with capital movement liberalization, since both are deriving from the accession calendar. In conclusion, full capital liberalization is likely to present Romania with the most important 'accession shock', but EU membership itself will provide cushions to alleviate this.

COMPETITION

The protection and even promotion of competition is inextricably intertwined with the goals of the Internal Market. Thus, the 'anti-trust' window of competition policy seeks to prevent private practices which attempt to divide up markets, thus effectively keeping them isolated (abuse of dominant positions, cartels etc), while the state aid window seeks to ensure that the increased competition brought by market integration is not distorted by state interventions propping up some companies to the detriment of others.

Though theoretically bound by the Europe Agreement to pursue a competition policy compatible with the one being applied in the EU, Romania has only very partially satisfied this commitment. The shortcomings were less visible in the area of anti-trust, where the risks of introducing distortions into the Internal Market are anyway limited, given that few, if any, companies under Romanian jurisdiction have the potential to engage in prohibited practices at the level of the European market. Moreover, in some cases the cure was arguably worse than the disease, in the sense that competition policy remedies applied by the competent national authority seem to have interfered with the requirement of free movement. There are at least two prominent examples. First, there was rejection, in the context of the control of economic concentrations, of several privatization transactions, based on flimsy grounds, which may well be regarded as (inadvertent) restrictions to the free movement of capital. Second, there is the recent conviction for abuse of dominant position by a company (KRONOSPAN) the only charge against which was an abrupt price increase. There was not even the suggestion that market contestability had been hampered in any way by its behaviour. The conviction can also be regarded as a case of indirect price control of the kind that falls foul of laws governing the free movement of goods.

The main problem area related to Romanian competition policy rests with state aids. While much emphasis has been put lately on the need to raise the capability and effectiveness of the national watchdog – the independent Competition Council – this may be the wrong target. Indeed, the main responsibility for dispensing incompatible state aids rests with the grantor – the government – which moreover is the one that assumed obligations in the context of both the Europe Agreement and the accession negotiations. Besides, since no national authority is competent for the vetting of state aids within the EU, where this area of regulation is exclusively supranational, there are limits to how many resources should be invested in a body which will soon have to give up its responsibilities in state aid matters. This view is vindicated by the fact that the net improvement of state aid discipline apparent since the beginning of 2005 is, first and foremost, a reflection of a much more moderate stance taken by the government in granting such aids.

The implications of unsatisfactory state aid control for the Internal Market should not be exaggerated, however. Although much larger in relative terms (percentage of value added), state aids granted in Romania are not very important in quantitative terms when compared to what existing member states are spending. Moreover, *prima facie* evidence exists of the lack of significant competitive distortions because, although entitled to countervailing actions against subsidized Romanian exports, EU manufacturers of like products have never made use of these in the 12 years since the entry into force of the trade part of the Europe Agreement.

Another aspect that should be considered when criticizing Romania's failure to implement a strict state aid control policy is that 'importing' at national level a system designed to deal with inter-state competitiveness is controversial. For instance, in the EU only the European Commission, as a neutral body and 'guardian of the Treaty', is able to identify the common interest which results from the combination of national interests not always convergent with one another. Supranational control is also justified by compelling political economy considerations, which make extremely unlikely the implementation of an effective state aid control 'at source', that is, by national authorities.

Strict state aid discipline, which will 'kick in' once Romania becomes a member of the EU, will undoubtedly entail a shock for those undertakings which are used to having easy access to subsidies. However, in view of the forms that these aids have taken so far, this shock should have mainly positive consequences. Indeed, most of the aids granted in Romania have consisted of debt cancellations (sometimes disguised as equity participations), which did nothing more than condone inefficiency and keep in the market manifestly unviable companies. Another widespread form of aids, which has been severely curtailed in the last two years, consisted of privileged tax treatment granted as part of a variety of schemes (e.g. disadvantaged areas, free zones, industrial parks, free ports, investments of 'significant dimension'). The illogical proliferation of such schemes led to a self-defeating situation whereby the tax base was eroded without even providing advantages to the recipients of the tax aids. This was because many of their competitors could have access to similar incentives by simply choosing another of the many venues available.

TAXATION

Besides discipline in the use of fiscal incentives, which is also part and parcel of the competition *acquis*, taking over the obligations of membership in the area of taxation entails the implementation of a harmonized indirect tax system. Romania has made progress in this respect mainly as concerns the non-discriminatory application of taxes (after having used excise duties, until as recently as 2003, as a vehicle for favouring domestic goods over their imported substitutes) and the harmonization of tax bases. It still has to repeal some incompatible VAT exemptions.

The remaining challenge is to gradually implement the minimum excise rates required by the acquis, against a background of current rates still being in some cases only a fraction of these minima (e.g., less than half for ethyl alcohol, about one third for cigarettes). It remains to be seen how tax revenues will be affected by the further increase of these taxes, taking into account the high elasticity of consumption and the limited administrative capacity, which increases the risk of tax fraud. On most energy products, however, the degree of approximation is higher and in some cases the mandatory minimum levels have already been reached.

This does not mean that energy price increases are no longer to be expected. For natural gas and, to a lesser extent, for electricity, price rises will still be implemented, but not so much in order to comply with the taxation *acquis*. Instead, the driving force behind this movement will be the application of sheer economic rationality principles, according to which prices must allow for the full recovery of costs. Higher energy prices will undoubtedly trigger adjustments in the economy, and some of them are already happening. A good example is the successive closure of most of Romania's production capacities for fertilizers. While some are lamenting this development, one should note that there was no reason in the first place for Romania, which is not a country rich in energy resources, to be a large producer and exporter of fertilizers, a very energy-intensive product.

CONCLUSION

The capacity to cope with the competitive pressures of the Internal Market is probably the most intriguing of the Copenhagen criteria. Indeed, it is difficult to understand how it is possible in economic terms *not* to cope with competition: resources will simply be reallocated to their more productive uses in the new context and efficiency should increase, though possibly with a lag due to adjustment. It is arguable that the significance of this criterion is political.

There are limits to how much a society might be willing to accept in terms of (short-term) costs even if the net ultimate outcome will be favourable. This also means that the degree of preparedness for EU accession is a very subjective undertaking, which at the end of the day hinges on the current perceptions of the evaluators – the European Commission – concerning the future perceptions of the Romanian people.

This chapter has argued that there are good reasons to discount the likelihood of a negative reaction from Romanian society to accession, because the shocks so induced will be far from dramatic. Much like Molière's *bourgeois gentilhomme*, Romania is already applying the *acquis communautaire* in many areas, even if the relevant actors do not always appreciate this. That said, some important changes still lay ahead. Three in particular should be noted in terms of the magnitude of their likely consequences: state aid discipline; the implementation of environmental directives; and unencumbered capital flows. Only positive consequences can flow from a tightening of state aid discipline. Unless one assumes that it would be possible not to enforce state aid rules in Romania, *while the other EU member states are not similarly exempted,* state aid discipline is a win-win undertaking, both in terms of classical comparative advantage and in terms of induced competitive advantage. Countries with 'larger pockets' than Romania's (i.e. almost all of them) would reap the benefits of the latter.

Adhering to the demanding environmental standards of the EU will undoubtedly bring some economic hardship but even in the worst-case scenario there is a silver lining. This will be the improved quality of the environment, something that the inhabitants of heavily polluted areas might come to value once they see that clean air and water can be made available to them as well.

The balance between the advantages of unhindered international capital movements and the costs of something going wrong is severely tilted in favour of the latter. Romania's macroeconomic situation is not so solid as to completely disregard the risk of a serious financial crisis, even if this risk is minimised by developments triggered by accession itself. However, unless one entertains baseless illusions about the possibility of having it both ways (i.e. acceding, yet without fully liberalizing the capital account), a clear-cut choice has to be made and it is difficult to see how a wholly precautionary approach may be preferred over early accession. This dilemma is, nevertheless, a good reminder of the fact that there is no gain without pain!

CHAPTER ELEVEN

Financial Services and EU Membership

Valentin Lazea

The Romanian financial sector is clearly dominated by the banking industry, with the capital market, insurance and pension funds playing a minor (albeit growing) role. The explanation for this has to do with history – banks continued to exist under the Communist regime, while the stock exchange was abolished – and with geography – Romania being closer to the Continental banks–based model than to the Anglo–Saxon one. Another possible explanation might be the less transparent way in which the first wave of privatizations was done, predominantly to insiders, through Management-Employee Buy-Outs (MEBOs) thus leaving little incentive for the new owners to go public. As a result, the banking industry is heavily involved in both the capital market and in the insurance industry, having established specialized branches which are leaders in these fields. The health of the banking system determines to a large extent therefore the soundness of the overall financial sector.

THE BANKING SYSTEM – HISTORICAL BACKGROUND

At the end of 1989, the banking system consisted of five state-owned banks, including the National Bank of Romania (NBR). Each of the other four specialized in a given sector: agriculture, foreign trade, investment, and house-hold savings. Each bank enjoyed a *de facto* monopoly and no competition existed. A reduced number of foreign banks' branches catered for specific markets.

A first reform entailed the splitting, in March 1991, of central bank activities (performed afterwards by the NBR) from commercial ones. These would now be the responsibility of a newly created bank, the Banca Comerciala Româna (BCR), in line with a new banking law and the NBR's statute. Starting in 1992, the NBR began issuing prudential regulations and exercising banking supervision. Monetary, inter-bank and foreign exchange markets were established. In 1993, a Banking College was set up to develop expertise so as to fill the chronic skills gap. In 1994, a first attempt to bring down inflation started bearing fruit, with the consumer price index (CPI) falling to 62% in December 1994 from 295% one year earlier. This was also the period when the first foreign entries (post-1989) were recorded, with the Dutch ING Bank and ABN-AMRO and the Turkish BTR and ROBANK setting foot in Romania. However, most foreign banks adopted a wait-and-see attitude and were reluctant to engage in what they perceived as a risky market, without any major privatization.

In 1995 the national payment system was improved through the opening of 42 clearing houses at the county level. However, transactions were still carried on manually in the absence of an Electronic Payment System (EPS). In the same year, the first law concerning bank bankruptcies was issued, but its emphasis was more on restructuring and less on orderly exit from the market. In 1996, the Deposit Guarantee Fund was established, covering all physical persons' deposits up to a certain amount.

However, during the first years of transition, the credit portfolio of the banks deteriorated massively. This was due to a range of reasons: a hostile macroeconomic environment, with high and unpredictable inflation and growing twin deficits; political interference in the banking industry, illustrated, among others, by direct credits granted on concessional terms to importers (through BANCOREX) and to farmers (through Banca Agricola); an unreformed microeconomic environment, dominated by still un-restructured state-owned borrowers; an obsolete accounting system, which in an environment of high inflation led to the de-capitalization of banks (the latter tried to protect themselves by investing in fixed assets rather than extending credit);poor legislation and even poorer enforcement (even in the happy case when assets were seized, the lack of a liquid market for them prevented the covering of the losses); and the lack of experience within the NBR in dealing with problems in the system (e.g. the lack of clear criteria for appointing bank managers and for confirming bank shareholders).

As a result, the credits classified as 'doubtful' and 'loss' kept increasing to 43.7% of the total in 1996, to 52.6% in 1997 and to 58.5% in 1998. By the end of 1998, the Romanian banking system was on the verge of collapse, with cumulative non-performing credits amounting to some 253% of own funds. As a result, a wave of bankruptcies resulted in the closure of five or six banks. The largest bank, BANCOREX ceased operations after its viable business had been transferred to BCR. Also, Banca Agricola underwent a very tough restructuring programme. All these measures cost the Romanian taxpayer

Table 11.1: Number of Romanian Commercial Banks and Foreign Bank
Branches

	1991	1995	2000	2005 (Q3)*
Commercial banks	11	24	33	33
state capital	6	7	4	2
private capital	5	17	29	31
majority foreign	0	8	21	24*
majority domestic	5	9	8	7*
Foreign banks' branches	5	7	8	6
Credit cooperatives	0	0	0	1
Total	16	31	41	40

Notes: * = Before BCR's privatization, which would increase the number of majority foreign private capital and decrease the number of majority domestic private capital by one unit, respectively.
Source: National Bank of Romania, *Annual Reports*, 2000-2004

almost 10% of GDP, without counting the additional costs to the Deposit Guarantee Fund, which were ultimately borne by the banks' clients.

In 1998–1999, the first bank privatizations took place, with the healthiest state-owned banks, BRD and Bancpost, being sold to, respectively, Société Generale of France and Euro Bank Ergasias of Greece. In the same period, the Austrian banks Bank Austria – Creditanstalt and Raiffeisenbank entered the Romanian market. Also in 1998, both major banking laws were amended and brought closer to European ones. A particular emphasis was put on strengthening the NBR's authorization and supervisory powers. A by-product of these was the establishment of a Credit Information Bureau and of a Payment Incident Bureau under the umbrella of the NBR.

Starting in December 1999, when Romania was officially invited to open accession negotiations with the European Union (EU), the emphasis shifted towards providing a stable macroeconomic environment and adopting the *acquis communautaire*. Indeed, inflation dropped from 40.7% in 2000 to 8.6% in 2005, while the budget deficit fell from 4.0% of GDP to 0.8% of GDP. Total public debt declined from 31.6% of GDP to less than 20% of GDP. The transposition of the *acquis* resulted in a new statute for the NBR (the third since 1989) which was adopted in the summer of 2004. It guarantees the full independence of the NBR and prohibits direct lending to the government. Also, a large array of secondary legislation (including supervision on a consolidated basis, supervision of credit co-operatives, of mortgage banks etc.) has been passed in recent years. The Deposit Guarantee Fund is gradually increasing both its coverage (extended to firms) and the amount to be covered, with the aim to reach the equivalent of €20,000 by 2007, the date of Romania's scheduled accession to the EU. Since 2001 several steps have been taken to liberalize capital account transactions. The most important of them – the opening by non-residents of local currency accounts with resident banks – took place in April 2005. The very last step – allowing non-residents access to money market instruments – is scheduled for September 2006.

In terms of the structure of the Romanian banking system, the privatizations of Banca Agricola (in 2001, with the Austrian Raiffeisenbank) and of BCR (in late 2005, with the Austrian Erste Bank) has led to a situation where more than 90% of banking assets are foreign-controlled. In this respect, Romania is similar to the most reform-minded countries of Central and Eastern Europe. The total number of banks has stabilized in the last few years around 40, the new entries being outweighed by the mergers and acquisitions of existing banks (see Table 11.1). A feature of the last few years is the appearance of specialized banks (for housing, for leasing, for micro-credits) in an environment dominated by universal banks. Also a degree of concentration of around 60% for assets, loans and own capital exists for the top five banks. This compares well with other countries in the region (see Table 11.2). In terms of foreign ownership, the Austrian banks were dominant even before BCR's privatization, followed by Greek, Italian and French banks (see Table 11.3). Prudential indicators have also witnessed a continuous improvement, as shown by the First Solvency Ratio, which is well above the threshold indicated by the Basle criteria (12%), or indeed, by the non-performing loans, which fell to 2.08% of own funds (see Table 11.4).

Beside BCR's privatization and (almost) full capital account liberalization, three notable events took place in 2005. First, there was the introduction of an EPS, allowing real-time settlements, a halving of the fees associated and a preparation for the participation in the European SEPA. Second the Romanian currency was redenominated from ROL to RON, or Romanian 'New' Leu, by slashing four zeroes and thus bringing it to a more 'European' value of 3.60 to €1. Third, there was the formal adoption of an inflation targeting framework. Although the 2005 target of 7.5% ± one percentage point was marginally missed (the CPI was 8.6%), there are a lot of good explanations for this, including the very bad agricultural year and the increase in international oil prices.

THE BANKING SYSTEM: CURRENT CHALLENGES

The Romanian banking system faces a number of important challenges. One of them represents the bill for delayed reforms and this can be explained in the

Table 11.2: Concentration Measured as the Share of Top Five Banks
(September 2005)

	% in total system
Assets	59.4
Loans	61.2
Government securities	52.2
Deposits	57.7
Own Capital	58.9

Source: National Bank of Romania, *Annual Reports*, 2000-2004

Table 11.3: Foreign Ownership, by Home Country (September 2005)*

Country	% in total foreign capital	% in total capital of the banking system
Austria	34.1*	25.1*
Greece	19.5	14.3
Italy	9.5	6.9
France	9.1	6.6
Netherlands	5.2	3.8
EBRD	4.5*	3.3*
Hungary	4.2	3.1
USA	3.0	2.2
IFC	2.6*	1.9*
Germany	2.1	1.5
Other countries	6.2	4.7
Total	100.0	73.4

Notes: * = before BCR's privatization, which would (more than) double the Austrian shares, while diminishing drastically those of EBRD and IFC.
Source: National Bank of Romania, *Annual Reports*, 2000-2004

following terms: while Romania has one of the lowest banking intermediations in Central and Eastern Europe, the rapid pace of credit growth poses significant challenges to the attaining of the inflation target. Indeed, Romania's bank intermediation is low even by South Eastern Europe (SEE) standards, with total banking assets representing less than 40% of GDP (compared to a SEE average of 58.2% of GDP) and with loans to non-government representing 18.4% of GDP in 2004 (22% of GDP in 2005) compared to a regional average of 30.3% of GDP. Moreover, loans per household are a mere €135, compared to Croatia's €1979 and to the region's €323 (see Table 11.5). No wonder, then, that the banks argue that there is plenty of room for rapid non-governmental credit growth. And rapidly it has grown indeed, increasing by an average 42.5% per

Table 11.4: Prudential Indicators for Commercial Banks

	1998	2000	2002	2005 (Q3)
1st Solvency Ratio (> 12%)	10.25	23.79	25.04	19.21
2nd Solvency Ratio (> 8%)	...	18.90	22.93	...
Past Due and Doubtful Claims/Own Capital	253.64	3.32	1.97	2.11
Return on Assets	0.06	1.49	2.64	2.09
Return on Equity	1.03	12.53	18.27	16.71

Source: National Bank of Romania, Annual Reports, 2000-2004

Table 11.5: Ratios in the SEE Banking Markets (2004)

	Total Assets (% of GDP)	Total loans		Loans to households (€ per capita)
		% of GDP	Annual Growth Rate (2000-2004)	
Albania	53.5	8.9	31.5	53
Bosnia-Herzegovina	72.6	45.2	18.2	352
Bulgaria	65.5	35.5	45.3	287
Croatia	108.9	61.7	21.3	1,979
Macedonia	56.7	17.3	15.5	112
Romania	38.3	18.4	42.5	135
Serbia	38.8	20.3	8.8	111
SEE	58.2	30.0	28.9	323
NMS	78.2	34.0	10.4	823
Eurozone	206.3	102.1	4.5	12,398

Source: Bank Austria Creditanstalt, Banking in South-Eastern Europe: On the move, September 2005

annum, between 2000 and 2004. However, this rate of growth significantly exceeds that of Croatia (21.3% p.a.) and of SEE as a whole (28.9% p.a.) and creates significant inflationary pressures, assuming increased domestic demand is not matched by increased domestic supply (and it is not!). Because of this threat, the NBR has issued several regulations, prudential in form but monetary in effect, trying to limit the non-government credit growth to a more manageable 20–30% per annum. One such example is the requirement, issued in 2005, for the banks not to extend foreign exchange credit in excess of 300% of their own funds. This makes it costly for the banks to pursue a very aggressive lending policy. Another important measure, which will come into effect in 2006, is the extension of NBR's supervision over non-bank financial institutions, such as leasing companies, which also contribute to the rapid expansion of credit and consumption.

A second challenge, closely related to the previous one, stems from the fact that, being foreign-owned, most banks find it easier to borrow resources from abroad, from their mother-banks, and to extend credits in foreign exchange, rather than go through the difficult process of attracting RON deposits as a source of local currency credit. At the end of 2004 the annual pace of growth for Euro credit was (in real terms) more than 90%, the annual pace of growth for Lei credit was (also in real terms) around 15%, with the overall credit growth averaging around 25%. However, NBR's measures succeeded to level off the rhythms of growth for Euro and for Lei, at around 60% (in real terms) each by December 2005. The measures included a further differentiation in Minimum Reserve Requirements (from 30% to 35% and, later, to 40% for foreign exchange deposits) while for Lei they were diminished from 18% to 16%. The increase in the share of Lei credit in total credit is necessary for two reasons. First, in monetary terms, an inflation targeting regime cannot properly work if the signal represented by changes in the domestic interest rate is transmitted to slightly less than half of the total credit, i.e. the domestic currency denominated one (currently, it stands at 10.2% of GDP, compared to 11.8% of GDP for the foreign exchange credit). Second, in prudential terms, the NBR has to alert borrowers who, attracted by the lower interest on foreign exchange credit, pay little attention to whether they are hedged or not in the same currency, while the banks prefer to turn a blind eye on the issue.

A third challenge for the Romanian banking system is to provide for enhanced competition, especially among larger banks. Despite very rapid credit growth, competition between banks for market share has been very weak until recently. One proof for this statement is the preservation of a very high margin between lending rates and deposit rates. Indeed, at the end of 2001, when inflation stood at around 30%, this margin was 14–15%. Four years later, with inflation having fallen to one-quarter of the previous value, the margin was still close to 10% (i.e. larger than inflation itself). A recent study by Lapteacru (2004), applying the Rosse-Panzar income test, finds that the banking system as a whole in Romania is characterised by monopolistic competition. While smaller banks compete fiercely in the market, the largest banks collude in an oligopolistic manner. As a result of this reduced competition, almost all foreign banks operating in Romania succeed in making hefty profits, some of the largest in the region.

A fourth challenge worth emphasizing is the very low banking exposure of particular areas and sectors. For instance, the rural area is very under-banked,

Table 11.6: Share of Alternative Sources of Financing for Non-Financial Sector Companies (2005) (in %)

	Own Capital	Domestic banking credit	External private debt	Other debt (commercial debt, bonds, arrears)
Agriculture	24.7	7.5	6.2	61.7
Industry and energy	43.4	5.3	6.3	44.9
Construction	25.5	7.0	3.5	64.0
Services and trade	21.0	5.9	5.5	67.6

Source: Mircea, R. et al *The role of Romanian non-financial companies in preserving financial stability*, mimeo, 2005

with only the Savings Bank (CEC) being present in around 800 of the more than 12,000 villages in Romania. Another 600 branches belong to the only network of credit co-operatives that has been authorized so far. The rest of the banks have hardly any presence especially in the towns that have less than 100,000 inhabitants. Therefore, the preservation of CEC's network following its privatization becomes a vital issue and it has been made one of the conditions which the new buyer will have to fulfil. On the other hand, sectors such as agriculture or tourism are completely under-banked, receiving around 2% of total credit each, despite their important potential for development. All these areas require a more proactive, risk-taking attitude on the part of commercial banks, which will only appear as a result of stronger competition. The other side of the coin shows that commercial companies are also reluctant to engage in banking credit, relying heavily for financing on internal resources and on other debt (commercial debt, bonds, arrears) (see Table 11.6). Hopefully, this attitude will also change with the fall in inflation and in the margins used by the banks.

OTHER FINANCIAL MARKETS: HISTORY AND CURRENT CHALLENGES

The opening in 1995 of the Bucharest Stock Exchange (BSE) was met with high hopes. Soon afterwards, it was followed by the establishment of RASDAQ, an over-the-counter stock exchange modelled on its American equivalent NASDAQ. The hopes proved to be unrealistic. With a privatization process based mainly on MEBOs and, in second place, on direct sales, the stock exchange had real difficulties in taking off. Therefore, in 2003 talks were initiated to unify the two existing institutions, BSE and RASDAQ, to a single

Table 11.7: Financial Indicators of the BSE and of RASDAQ (2000 - 2004)

	2000	2001	2002	2003	2004
Number of listed companies					
BSE	114	65	65	62	60
RASDAQ	5382	5084	4823	4442	3998
Capitalization (€ million)					
BSE	450	1361	2646	2991	8818
RASDAQ	872	1188	1764	1943	2064
Transaction rate (TR, %)					
BSE	21.3	15.8	10.4	9.6	10.3
RASDAQ	16.0	9.9	9.1	5.8	8.2
Price/Earning Ratio (PER)					
BSE	3.98	4.92	9.12	13.10	35.18
RASDAQ	1.52	2.95	3.03	4.17	6.58

Source: National Commission for Securities, *Annual Report*, 2004

one. However, the years 2004 and 2005 witnessed an increased appetite especially from foreign investors, due to Romania's forthcoming accession into the EU. Both the capitalization and the efficiency indicators of the two markets increased tremendously (see Table 11.7).

The first challenge that this market has to overcome is linked to the relatively small number of liquid shares. Currently, only around 20 companies are liquid enough and belong to the first tier. Among them, there are three banks, two oil companies and some pharmaceutical companies. It is expected that the liquidity of the market will increase after the listing of some energy sector companies. A second problem is with the relatively small number of institutional investors. As long as pension reform is still lagging, there is also a lack of pension funds which would give added weight to the market. Third, it remains to be seen how much of the recent exceptional growth of BSE was linked to fundamentals or was rather an asset bubble, prompted by the negative real interest rates of the NBR in its attempt to fight speculative capital inflows. All in all, the Romanian stock exchanges are characterized by high volatility, which might be good for speculators, but less so for institutional investors. There is a hope that EU accession will change this. A promising development might also be the trading of municipal bonds, a largely untapped market with high potential, which will be stimulated by EU funds.

The insurance market has also been growing rapidly only in the last few years. Major international players, such as ING Nederlanden, Generali, Unita,

AIG, are present in the Romanian market. The latter has increased its value threefold in the last five years, reaching around €1.27 billion in 2005, with a growth of 40% over the previous year. Around 40 insurance companies are present, with their activity regulated by the Commission for Insurance Supervision. Banks' branches take the lion's share, selling some 25% of the total insurance. This activity, called 'bank assurance' has been developed in different ways in Europe: while in the UK only 15% of insurance is sold through banks, in countries such as France, Italy or Spain the percentage can go to 60-80%. Romania will, most likely, follow this second model. One of the challenges faced by this market is the need for further consolidation. Thus, from 42 insurance companies operating in 2004, only 28 registered profit, while 14 posted losses.

Another major challenge is the lack of a reinsurance company in Romania, all the reinsurance being done by non-resident companies. This might be a problem especially for a country with a high risk of seismic activity, such as Romania, where many old buildings would be damaged by an earthquake. House insurance is not mandatory and is discouraged by the low level of disposable income.

The reform of the pension system in Romania consists of two components: the parametric reform of the pay-as-you-go system, also known as the first pillar (state and mandatory) and the introduction of the second pillar (private and mandatory), while the third pillar (private and optional) is already offered by insurance companies. Whereas the first component was enacted in April 2001 through the new Public Pensions Law, the second component was repeatedly postponed. The second pillar will probably become operational in 2007, with an important effect on the capital market as well.

Looking at the financial sector as a whole, one can notice the following three major challenges. First, its components are unevenly developed, both in terms of volume and readiness of competition within the EU. Second, banks are exposed in all sectors, through specialized branches; for the time being, the risk of contagion is limited, but it could grow over time, if co-operation between the supervisory bodies is found wanting. Third, the current macroeconomic environment, which stimulates growth through consumption, is hurting not only the banking sector (via lower incentives for saving), but also the other financial markets, especially the long-term oriented ones, such as the insurance market. Prudent macroeconomic policies will be therefore be of vital importance for financial services not only in the lead-up to Romania's accession to the EU but also crucially thereafter too,

SOURCES

Bank Austria Creditanstalt, *Banking in South-Eastern Europe: On the move*, September 2005

Commission for Insurance Supervision, *Annual Reports*, 2000-2004

European Bank for Reconstruction and Development, *Transition Report 2005: Business in Transition*, 2006

Lapteacru, I. *The structure of Romanian banking industry*, mimeo, 2004

Mircea, R. et al *The role of Romanian non-financial companies in preserving financial stability*, mimeo, 2005

National Bank of Romania, *Annual Reports*, 2000-2004

National Commission for Securities, *Annual Reports*, 2000-2004

CHAPTER TWELVE

The Common Foreign and Security Policy: What Can Romania Bring?

Mihai-Răzvan Ungureanu

One can argue that Romania has been a contributor to the Common Foreign and Security Policy (CFSP) for a long time. Since 1 February 1993, when Romania signed its Europe Agreement with the European Union (EU), the fourth Central and East European (CEE) country to do so, Romanian and EU officials have developed an increasingly active dialogue on foreign policy issues. At the beginning, according to the Europe Agreement, the dialogue was limited to 'international issues of common interest' and was conducted at expert or ministerial level. Subsequently, the dialogue was extended to the level of Heads of State and Government. Over the years, the dialogue evolved swiftly, taking place with increased frequency and depth. It has always been a two-way street, allowing Romania both to better understand EU positions and to offer opinions and insights into foreign policy areas of particular interest.

For some years now, Romania has associated itself with all CFSP positions and statements adopted and issued by the EU. The foreign policy chapter of the *acquis* was the first to be closed during the accession negotiations. Since 25 April 2005, when the Accession Treaty was signed, Romania – as an active observer – has had a voice, though not a vote, and has tried to make use of this status to the full. Romania has contributed in particular with regards to its immediate neighbourhood – Eastern Europe and the Western Balkans – and to the operational dimension of the European Security and Defence Policy (ESDP), participating directly in EU missions in the Balkans and in the Middle East area.

When Romania joins the EU, it will bring to the table a predictable foreign policy with an extensive expertise particularly on the neighbouring regions.

It is also in Romania's direct interest to participate in the CFSP, contributing not only to the strengthening of the role of the EU in the world but also to promoting from a larger and stronger forum her own foreign policy agenda. On the other hand, after years of increasingly closer interaction with the EU, Romania is fully aware of the EU's positions, joint actions, common strategies and other CFSP-related instruments. It is worth mentioning that both the European Commission and the member states have agreed that CFSP provisions are fully harmonized and implemented in Romania.

Over the years, Romania's contributions to the CFSP have been highly significant. In various cases Romania's activity was either aligned to or actively helped shape EU policy. Several examples are worth noting: Romania's Chairmanship of the Organization for Security and Cooperation in Europe (OSCE), in 2001, which was run in close consultation with the EU and in line with the EU's foreign policy; the conduct of high-level Romanian officials in fora such as the Stability Pact for South-Eastern Europe; Romania's membership of the South-East European Cooperation Process (SEECP); and Romania's membership of the UN Security Council in 2004–2005.

The premise of a continuous Romanian contribution to the EU, to its foreign policy in particular, even in the pre-accession stage is obviously true. Nowhere is this clearer than in the area of the ESDP. Since long before accession to the EU, Romania has been taking part in ESDP missions and operations such as the European Union Police Mission (EUPM) and the European Union Military Operation (Althea) in Bosnia-Herzegovina, Concordia in the Former Yugoslav Republic of Macedonia, and most recently the European Union Border Assistance Mission at the Rafah Crossing Point in the Palestinian Territories (EU BAM Rafah) and the EU Police Mission for the Palestinian Territories (EU COPPS).

WILL ACCESSION MEAN JUST A CONTINUATION OF ROMANIA'S CONTRIBUTION TO CFSP?

The example of the ten new member states that joined the EU in 2004 shows that, once a candidate joins, it gains a new confidence and assertiveness in its contribution to the CFSP. Membership is a fertile ground for promoting foreign policy issues of national interest or, more often, for activism in areas of particular expertise.

Since the first batch of CEE countries joined the EU, there has obviously been renewed interest at EU level in relations with Ukraine, the Republic of Moldova, Belarus, and other former Soviet Republics, based on the better understanding of and interaction with that region that the newcomers have.

In addition, expertise on the Western Balkans within the EU has been increased. Like all previous new members, Romania will bring to the EU its own windows to the outside world, its own areas of specific expertise, as well as the force of arguments in areas of vital national interest.

ROMANIA'S CONTRIBUTION AND PRIORITIES

Romania's experience in a number of fora will contribute to the country's profile as a new EU member state. It was the Chair-in-Office of the OSCE in 2001, organized a successful OSCE Ministerial meeting in Bucharest, is a member of a multitude of regional organizations, has held the rotating chair in all of them, been a member of the UN Security Council (in 1990–1991 and 2004–2005), and chaired the Council of Ministers of the Council of Europe (2005–2006). As a relatively large new member state, the seventh in terms of size and population, Romania will bring to the EU a large diplomatic service, with an impressive number of embassies, consulates and honorary consulates. It will also bring a diplomatic service that has a tradition of excellence.

Romania – which will be part of the EU's external border – will be interested, as it has been so far, in the stability, democracy and prosperity of *neighbouring countries*, particularly those outside the EU, namely the Republic of Moldova, Ukraine, those in the wider Black Sea Area, and those in the Western Balkans.

A priority dimension that Romania will promote relates to the Republic of Moldova, a neighbouring country which shares centuries of history as well as culture with Romania. Not only do trade, economics and culture link the people in Romania and the Republic of Moldova but so too do ties of kinship. Relations between the people living on the two sides of the border between the two countries are special and indestructible. As a result, it is natural that Romania will continue to plead, from inside the EU, for support for a settlement of the Transnistrian conflict, for addressing the threats to regional stability and security arising from the region, for Moldova's prosperity, and for an increasingly closer relationship with the EU. As a member, Romania's support for the Republic of Moldova will continue and focus on new areas. From within the EU, Romania will advocate a continuation of the EU's involvement in the democratisation of Transnistria, the region east of the river Nistru. EU involvement, particularly via the activity of the EU Special Representative for Moldova, the deployment of the European Union Border Assistance Mission to Moldova and Ukraine, and the EU's participation in the negotiations on the status of Transnistria, will be supported by Romania. Strong support will also be given to the shaping of a clearer European perspective for the Republic of Moldova along with the countries of the Western Balkans, a vision which would include a credible European policy towards this country.

Ukraine, a key country to the North and East of Romania, will also be the focus of Romania's contributions to the CFSP. On the basis of its own experience in democratic transition, alongside that of other new member states, Romania will continue to work with others in the EU to shape democratic developments in Ukraine, to support the authorities in Kiev to bring stability, democracy and prosperity to the Ukrainian people, and to promote Ukraine's Europeanness both internally and in the country's relations with its neighbours. In this respect, Romania is committed to making use of the opportunity of solving – together with Ukraine and the international organisations already involved – the Bystroe issue.[1] This is not a bilateral problem, but a European one: the Danube Delta is an invaluable and internationally important asset. And it is important to further promote unconditional respect for international environmental law in the region.

At the same time, Romania will be mindful of the need for Ukrainians to understand the extent of the domestic political and economic transformation that needs to occur. It will not spare any efforts in order to make sure that Ukraine takes a path to democracy and a better life similar to that taken by all other CEE countries during the last fifteen years. Following regime change in Kiev, and as proof of its support for its neighbour's European path, Romania is ready to help Ukraine meet her EU and Council of Europe commitments, trustful that one day the two countries will both be part of a prosperous and democratic EU.

One important lesson that Romania has learnt during its transition concerns the oft-discussed issue of national minorities. Although reluctant in this respect in early 1990s, Romanian authorities have since understood in depth what 'respect for and protection of national minorities' means. The attention paid by the EU to this matter has been a real support for the improvement of democratic standards and respect for human rights and fundamental freedoms, of which minority rights are a natural part. Romania is now in the position to share this experience with countries from our eastern neighbourhood and from the Western Balkans, and we are truly in the position to argue that minority rights are not part of a hidden agenda, as conspiracy theories often maintain, but a very helpful

---

[1]   *Editor's note.* The Ukrainian Bystroe Project concerns the creation of a navigation channel in the central part of the Danube Delta. Aimed at boosting the economy in the region, it has raised considerable concern internationally regarding its likely negative environmental impact on the Delta, which is protected under the UNESCO Man and Biosphere Programme. For further details, see: http://europa.eu.int/comm/environment/enlarg/bystroe_project_en.htm.

tool for democratisation. The presence of Romanian-speaking communities in neighbouring countries will ease this effort, as they shall be a natural bridge between our countries. Romania wishes to promote this idea and ensure that the rights of ethnic Romanian living in Ukraine meet European standards. The situation of the Romanian minority in Ukraine is a legitimate and natural preoccupation of Romania which is looking forward to making use of common historical Romanian-Ukrainian links in order to establish a show case of bilateral cooperation in this area. The position of Romanian communities in Ukraine, Serbia, Albania or Macedonia will be, from our perspective, one more argument for speeding up the EU accession of these countries.

It should not be forgotten that Romania is constantly pleading, and will continue to do so, for a thorough implementation of the European Neighbour-hood Policy (ENP), which it regards as a special opportunity for consolidating the EU's relations with some of its Eastern neighbours. Romania has expressed, on various occasions, her readiness to support the translation into practice of the EU Action Plans with the Republic of Moldova and Ukraine, starting with the immediate priorities identified by these two neighbours as well as with forms of support that Romania can offer. In Romania's view, a positive evaluation in the process of implementation of Action Plans will build up the EU's rapprochement with the Republic of Moldova and Ukraine and will represent the basis for an enhanced future relationship between the EU the these countries.

The wider Black Sea Area should not be overlooked too. It is already a region of interest to the EU. With the accession of Romania and Bulgaria the EU will for the first time have among its membership two littoral countries. It will also have a third, Turkey, engaged in accession negotiations. Russia has its own strategic partnership with the EU, and together they are trying to build four common spaces. The remaining countries of the region – Ukraine, the Republic of Moldova, Georgia, Azerbaijan and Armenia – are part of the ENP. The EU is already an actor in the region with a significant capacity to support the littoral countries in their struggle for democratisation, security and prosperity.

Potentially Romania (and Bulgaria) will have the biggest impact on the CFSP with regard to the Black Sea region. Although the EU does not have a common strategy towards the Black Sea area yet and until recently, the region was, in many respects, *terra incognita* for EU officials, Romania is convinced that EU efforts should and will be stepped up in the region as its significance increases almost daily. The Black Sea area is vital for the EU's future energy security, particularly as a link to the Caspian Sea and Central Asia. It is also important in terms of sea transport being linked to the heart of the European continent via the longest European waterway, the Danube. As an eco-system, the Black Sea area has the potential to influence all of Europe. From an environmental point of view, the Black Sea area is a great opportunity for European research and action. In terms of flows of traffic of persons, drugs and conventional arms, the region is at the crossroads of all major routes. Moreover, the Black Sea region has the potential to become an excellent test-case for EU-Russia cooperation, probably with US involvement as well. The logic of regarding the countries as a region is compelling despite the many differences that exist between them. Eventually, the Black Sea might become an internal EU sea once Turkey joins and if the other EU neighbours continue their quest for closer relations with the EU and complete the reforms necessary to achieve this.

It is precisely the wider Black Sea Area where Romania sees a potential for further ESDP involvement. There are four frozen conflicts – in the Republic of Moldova over Transnistria, in Georgia over Abkhazia and South Ossetia, and between Armenia and Azerbaijan over Nagorno-Karabakh – that have already lasted for too long. They affect not only security and stability, but undermine the natural development of the states concerned. The OSCE has not been very successful in dealing with these conflicts. The EU appears to many of the affected countries as an honest peace broker. It also has the capability to provide peaceful solutions: it is in a privileged position with regard to Russia and has at its disposal a variety of political, military and civilian instruments for implementing post-settlement measures.

As previously highlighted, the Black Sea will be a test-case for the EU, not least from the security/defence point of view: it is an area where the EU might prove unequivocally its status as a provider of peace and stability. In the conflicts of the Black Sea Region, we see the EU involved at all levels of the settlement process, we see the EU interacting with Russia and we see an opportunity for the EU to combine military and civilian instruments in joint civil-military operations. These are the type of operations, based on experience and the lessons learned from previous actions, for which the EU provides real added value that can generate change.

As for participation in *regional organisations*, Romania has been active in the initiatives and activities promoted by the Stability Pact for South-Eastern Europe and is playing a significant role in the SEECP, the South-East European Defence Ministerial and other fora. The regional centre of the Southeast European Cooperation Initiative (SECI), based in Bucharest, is the first regional attempt to exchange information on transit at borders aimed at deterring, detecting and addressing illegal traffic. Once Romania joins the EU, the centre will be located in an EU capital. As such it will act as a powerful reminder to the countries of the Western Balkans that the EU is committed to enlargement to include South-Eastern Europe provided the countries in the region undertake the necessary reforms. Being one of the initiators of the Danube Cooperation Process, together with Austria, the European Commission and the Stability Pact for South-Eastern Europe, Romania will make use of this unique forum of cooperation as a supplementary tool to achieve the goals of EU policies for the Western Balkans and the ENP the area. The Danube will, after all, become, almost entirely, an internal river of the EU once Romania and Bulgaria join.

Trans-Atlantic Relations: As a member on the external border of both the EU and the North Atlantic Treaty Organization (NATO), Romania will consistently plead for a constructive, effective and close transatlantic relationship. In order to address in the most proper and effective way the challenges the international environment raises, Romania will advocate close coordination and coherence between EU and US actions, as well as for stronger partnership between EU and NATO. Romania will bring to the EU, as it already does to NATO, the profile of a European ally with a Euro-Atlantic vocation, a firm supporter of mutually reinforcing NATO and EU roles in Euro-Atlantic and international security issues.

On EU-NATO relations Romania shares the view that the two organizations should provide complementary frameworks for enhanced national contributions to common security and common defence. In military terms, Romania's NATO membership brought a higher defence budget (around 3% of GDP), a defence reform and new and better capabilities able to act according to the tasks of the Alliance. These evolutions are mirrored by our involvement in the ESDP, even before accession. Romania participates in two battlegroups, will use the ESDP framework for developing civilian capabilities with a view to civilian or civil-military operations and will use the opportunity of the European Defence Agency to develop its defence and defence R&D programmes. So far, efforts made through integration with the EU and NATO are clearly mutually reinforcing and they should remain like that.

In political terms, we view NATO as the forum for dialogue on strategic issues with our American partners. Of course, NATO needs substantial reforms, but the aforementioned principle should remain unaltered. Political will from the leaders of member states and allied states is crucial in this context and will be crucial in the future should ESDP develop further. Romania supported the changes envisaged in the EU's Constitutional Treaty in the area of the CFSP and ESDP and hopes to see them reflected in reality. Should the political will be lacking, the changes proposed and, not the least, needed, would though put additional pressure on EU-NATO relations.

The future of the CFSP: At the political, economic and military level, Romania is pursuing a direct contribution to the development of the ESDP, having had the opportunity to join this comprehensive process right from the start. The main guiding principle in its endeavours is advance planning in order to respond to new challenges and to keep up with organizations which themselves transform. This is the only way to ensure that future EU membership will bring an added value into the long-term investment in European stability. In the same vain, and closely linked to the EU's interests, Romania brings to the EU table a history of close relations and cooperation with important non-European countries, such as China, India and Pakistan, the nations of the Middle East, Africa and Latin American countries.

For instance, Romania has traditionally good relations with countries in the Middle East and Maghreb, based on political ties, economic cooperation, trade exchanges and human connections – there are small communities of Romanians living in these countries, and there are Muslims living in Romania as well, perfectly integrated. Romania can thus be a 'resonance box' for European values in the Middle East and foster dialogue between cultures and religions, whether within the Euro-Mediterranean framework, through the likes of the Anna Lindh Foundation, or using other fora.

To conclude, Romania wants to be a trusted, reliable, active partner, a promoter of an increasingly *common* foreign and security policy, a facilitator of consensus, an actor that contributes positively to the assertiveness of the EU as a global player. It is difficult to assess, before accession, however, the potential impact that Romania joining the EU will have on the CFSP. What is clear is that Romania will be an additional driving force behind efforts to achieve the EU's objectives regarding foreign and security policy. It will also be an advocate for greater EU involvement in key regions, both in the EU's immediate vicinity and further afar.

Romania, Enlargement and the
New Neighbours

CHAPTER THIRTEEN

Romania, the Black Sea and Russia

Sergiu Celac

In an earlier essay, I tried to identify the converging interests of the West – meaning primarily the European Union (EU) and the United States – in the wider Black Sea region as there are so many compelling reasons for developing a transatlantic strategy for that part of the world.[1] The rationale for Romania's interest and increasing activism in the region is of more immediate and obvious nature.

First of all, Romania is there, one of the six Black Sea littoral states, with specific interests and policy objectives deriving from the simple fact of geography. A combination of location, economic interdependence, cultural affinity and historical experience, good or bad, has shaped over time Romania's complex web of interaction with its neighbours and its distinctive place in regional affairs.

National security concerns rank high on the Black Sea agenda of the current Romanian government. The prevailing situation in the region is seen as 'an accumulation of negative energies',[2] with active or dormant hotbeds of tension extending in an arc of crisis from the Western Balkans northward to Transnistria and all the way to the North and South Caucasus. The combustible mix of old and new dangers to regional stability, including also the spread of organised crime, based mainly, but not exclusively, in unrecognised and unaccountable 'rogue' entities, and increased trafficking in drugs and other prohibited materials, weapons and human beings, is perceived as a direct threat to the national security of Romania. An adequate response to these challenges

---

[1] Celac, S. 'Five Reasons Why the West Should Become More Involved in the Black Sea Region', in Asmus, R.D. et al (eds) *A New Euro-Atlantic Strategy for the Black Sea Region* (Washington D.C.: German Marshall Fund, 2004), pp. 138–146.

[2] See the talk of Traian Băsescu, President of Romania, to students and faculty at the University of Bucharest, 14 June 2005, verbatim transcript via www.ziua.ro, 15 July 2005.

requires, according to the Romanian President, making the Black Sea a top priority of the country's foreign policy, promoting concerted action at a regional level, and encouraging a positive involvement of the international community in the region. In this vision, the three main pillars of a new regional strategy are the internationalisation of the Black Sea problematique, continued efforts for the democratisation and modernisation of the region's countries, and further development of a mindset for and the structures of cooperative regionalism.[3]

The broader trends in the evolution of international circumstances and the dynamics of regional developments are considered to be propitious to such a novel approach. As the old fears begin to recede into oblivion and are gradually replaced by a growing awareness of promising opportunities, regional actors are apt to see merit in a constructive, rather than confrontational, stance and to decide in favour of cooperation as a matter of enlightened self-interest. The same line of reasoning is likely to motivate, it is hoped, other institutional actors, the EU in particular, in their own designs for the Black Sea region, notably in those areas where major, long-term strategic interests are involved. To illustrate the point, if current trends persist, the EU's dependency on imported energy is expected to climb from 50% in 2000 to over 70% in 2030 (90% for oil, 80% for gas, 66% for coal), with about half of the supply crossing the Black Sea space from original sources north and east of it.[4] It is assumed that, rather than dealing separately with its individual eastern neighbours, as has been the case so far, the EU may eventually decide to take a new look at the region as a coherent entity.

Romania sees a role for itself in this process. It is well placed to understand how high the stakes for Europe are in matters of energy security and the safety of related infrastructure since it is an oil and gas producer, importer and transit country itself. The ambitious goals of the emerging South-East European Energy Community, in which Romania is an active participant, are regarded as a possible test case for a broader European energy strategy. Equally important for the long-term interests of the EU and its eastern neighbours is the comprehensive development of combined and multi-modal transport infrastructure in line with the agreed concept of pan-European corridors. Viewed from Bucharest, all these elements, in addition to broader political considerations, strongly argue in favour of positive steps toward developing a new regional dimension of EU policies with a focus on the Black Sea area, comparable and complementary to the existing schemes for the Mediterranean, the North (through the Northern Dimension), and the Western Balkans.

---

[3]   Ibid.
[4]   Geopolitics of EU Energy Supply, *EurActiv*, 22 July 2005 (via www.euractiv.com).

In the view of the Romanian government, the Black Sea Economic Cooperation (BSEC) has an important part to play as a catalyst for a new regional identity and a reliable interlocutor for other regional and international partners. Founded on 25 June 1992, the BSEC now comprises twelve member states and is endowed with the complete institutional structure of a full-fledged regional organisation (Council of Ministers of Foreign Affairs, a Permanent International Secretariat, sectoral working groups, parliamentary assembly, regional bank, business council, and a think tank – the International Centre for Black Sea Studies). Although the actual accomplishments in the BSEC's core business of economic cooperation have been less than satisfactory,[5] significant progress has been made in other areas (e.g. justice and home affairs, science and technology) and in streamlining operational practices and procedures in a multilateral format, thus laying a solid groundwork for future cooperative action. A founding member of the BSEC, Romania has been moderately active and has occasionally shown interest in its work, with punctual contributions in such areas as regional security and stability or combating organised crime and international terrorism.[6] There are indications, however, that, given the prominence of the Black Sea on the current government's agenda, a more pro-active attitude toward the BSEC may be in the making. In a statement released on the occasion of the 13th anniversary of the BSEC, the Ministry of Foreign Affairs of Romania highlighted the priorities of the forthcoming Romanian Chairmanship-in-Office of the organisation (November 2005-April 2006): to promote closer cooperation among member states, to enhance the regional and international visibility of the BSEC, and to upgrade dialogue with the EU with the aim of developing a meaningful partnership.[7] To that end, it is envisaged that a focus will be on encouraging the implementation of projects having a region-wide impact, expanding cooperative interaction with other international organisations, and stepping up the reform process within the BSEC itself in order to enable it to respond more effectively to regional challenges in a wider international context.

With an eye on EU membership, hopefully as of 1 January 2007, Romania has incorporated specific regional responsibilities in its pre-accession strategy, in addition to the absorption of the *acquis communautaire* and the creation of appropriate implementation mechanisms. Foremost among these are the proper

[5] For a critique of BSEC's performance in the economic sphere, see Manoli, P. 'Limited Integration: Transnational Exchanges and Demands in the BSEC Area', *Agora without Frontiers* (special issue), 10 (4) 2005 (via www.idec.gr/iier/new/tomos10/MANOLI.pdf).
[6] A comprehensive review of Romanian initiatives within the BSEC and its related bodies can be found on the official website (www.mae.ro) of the Ministry of Foreign Affairs of Romania.
[7] *Rompres*, special release, 30 June 2005 (via www.rompres.ro).

management of the EU's external borders, considering that three of Romania's immediate neighbours – Ukraine, Moldova and Serbia and Montenegro – are not likely to join the EU at least in the next few years, in parallel with a constructive opening in bilateral relations in line with the European Neighbourhood Policy and other EU policy instruments. The diversity of BSEC membership in terms of international affiliation is seen in this context as an asset rather than a liability, offering the possibility of an institutionalised partnership for the promotion of shared values and for undertaking major projects with a regional impact.

Romania's renewed Black Sea activism seems to extend well beyond the framework of the BSEC and to find an articulate expression in a variety of diplomatic initiatives and demarches in other international fora as well. As an elected, non-permanent member of the United Nations (UN) Security Council for 2004–2006, Romania initiated a debate on the substance of UN cooperation with regional organisations in stabilisation processes. A formal resolution to that effect was adopted during the second round of the Romanian rotating presidency of the Council, in October 2005.[8]

Constructive involvement in regional affairs with a special focus on the wider Black Sea area is also seen as part of Romania's duties as a responsible member of NATO and a future member of the EU, and as a demonstration of its willingness and ability to produce value added for its allies and partners. There is a clearer awareness now in Bucharest that fostering normal bilateral relationships with immediate neighbours at the eastern edge of the EU and the Atlantic Alliance is an asset for Romania itself and makes a positive contribution to a new European architecture of security and cooperation.[9] A case in point is presented by the new developments in Romania's relations with the Russian Federation.

The collapse of communism and the dissolution of the Soviet Union brought about a new, unexpected situation with far-reaching implications for Russo-Romanian relations: for the first time in centuries Romania – and for that matter its predecessor the Danubian Principalities – no longer shares a common border with Russia. But even in the new circumstances the full normalisation of bilateral relations was slow to materialize mainly because of the complex nature of historical legacy and the emotional and psychological charge of past experiences. Romania was among the last Central European countries to sign, on 4 July 2003, and ratify, in 2004, a Treaty on Friendly Relations and

---

[8] UN Security Council, *Resolution 1631 (2005)*, 17 October 2005 (available via www.un.org/News/Press/docs/2005/sc8526.doc.htm. For background, see Mihai-Răzvan Ungureanu, Minister of Foreign Affairs of Romania, interview with *Ziua*, 10 August 2005.

[9] Băsescu, *op. cit.*

Cooperation with the Russian Federation. The process took more than twenty rounds of negotiations and registered two failed attempts to produce an agreed text (in 1991 and 1996) that could be safely ratified according to the established constitutional procedures. For the two outstanding issues that were of crucial importance to the Romanian side – the condemnation of the Molotov-Ribbentrop Pact of 1939 and the situation of the Romanian gold bullion and other treasure deposited for safekeeping in Russia in 1916–1917 – a compromise solution was eventually found in a Joint Declaration of the two Foreign Ministers, which was annexed to the Treaty.

A brief look at the calendar of mutual contacts, since 1990, at the level of high officials of state (presidents, prime ministers, speakers of Parliament, ministers of foreign affairs) indicates that most of the visits to Moscow had a working character, while most of the visits to Bucharest were tied to participation in multilateral events (OSCE, BSEC, etc.).[10] The political messages exchanged on those occasions, especially after the conclusion of the Treaty on Friendly Relations and Cooperation, were cautiously optimistic. On his first official visit to the Russian Federation, on 14 February 2005, Romanian President Traian Băsescu was reported to have told President Vladimir Putin: 'I am convinced that we can talk of our bilateral relations in the future tense; the past is a reality but my country wants to look into future'.[11] Echoing the encouraging results of those talks, the Russian Ambassador to Bucharest subsequently stated: 'We are prepared to go in our relations with Romania as far as Romania itself is prepared to go. For us there are no limits'.[12]

Still, a persistent issue in the Romanian-Russian political dialogue is the continued unauthorized presence of Russian forces and military equipment in the breakaway Transnistria province of the Republic of Moldova, quite close to the Romanian border. On this particular point Romania has consistently supported the sovereignty, unity and territorial integrity of Moldova and has advocated a European solution for that 'frozen conflict' through a more active, hands-on involvement of the EU, because 'when the EU is involved, Romania is also involved'.[13]

In their official pronouncements and public statements, both sides currently tend to emphasize the positive prospects of bilateral cooperation in a pragmatic, future-oriented approach. At the 6th session of the bilateral Intergovernmental Commission for Economic and Scientific-Technological Cooperation (Bucharest,

---

[10] 'Romania-Russia Relations: Documentary File', *Rompres* (via www.rompres.ro, accessed 10 August 2005).
[11] 'Basescu isi lasa mobilul deschis pentru Putin', *Evenimentul zilei*, 15 February 2005.
[12] Alexandr Tolkach, interview for *Russia la zi*, cited in *Ziua*, 21 June 2005.
[13] Traian Băsescu, interview for the newspaper *Gazeta Românească*, Chisinau, 4 July 2005.

7–8 July 2005) it was noted that mutual trade exchanges amounted to US$2.3 billion in 2004 and were poised to exceed US$3 billion in 2005.[14] The imbalance, however, is striking. While almost 7% of Romania's imports (mainly oil and gas and other commodities) come from Russia, Romanian exports to Russia are struggling around $100 million per annum. The problem has been aggravated by rising prices for hydrocarbons. Both sides take this situation seriously, not least because it inhibits further Romanian imports of Russian technology and industrial equipment, but so far the results have been below expectations and certainly behind Romania's competitors from Central Europe. There is an increasing interest on the part of the Romanian business community to recover some of the positions once held in the now very competitive Russian markets and to develop more active commercial ties with local partners in various regions of Russia.

The improved substance and quality of the intellectual debate in Romania on the present state and the prospects of Russo-Romanian bilateral relations is an encouraging recent development. In a deliberate oversimplification of the issue, while calling for a more nuanced approach, a Bucharest newspaper classified the Romanian attitudes toward Russia: 'some still see it as an evil empire, some are nostalgic about communist times, and some are only in love with Russian culture and arts'.[15] Similar clichés are also occasionally encountered in the Russian popular press when it comes to Romania and the Romanians. Moving away from such entrenched stereotypes, current debates tend to focus more realistically on specific issues and to seek workable solutions rather than engage in emotional dissertations about past grievances. The political analyst, Stelian Tănase, for example, has commented: 'Denial of reality, to my mind, appears to be the worst thing we can do', while the columnist Emil Hurezeanu has noted that 'We [Romanians] still lack powerful ideas for immediate and positive communication on the relations between Romania and Russia'.[16]

---

[14] Mark Abarsalin, Trade Commissioner of the Russian Federation to Romania, statement to *Rusia la zi*, 9 July 2005.

[15] 'Relatiile romano-ruse, sub semnul intrebarii mult timp, se destin', *Gardianul*, 29 July 2004.

[16] See also the comments of Adrian Severin, former Foreign Minister, that 'There is no inconsistency – rather the reverse is true – between our pro-NATO and pro-EU policies, and a strong and healthy relationship with the Russian Federation'; of the historian Florin Constantiniu that 'One can hardly discuss our modern history without a thorough knowledge of the Russian language, archives and historiography'; and the former deputy Prime Minister, Mircea Coşea that 'We have long regarded the Russian market as an inferior one related to Romania's economic capability; that has eventually turned against us'. Cited in 'Rusia, o lume uitata' (verbatim transcript of a round-table debate), *Ziua*, 12 June 2003 (via www.ziua.ro).

Slowly but steadily, both countries seem to be moving toward a more constructive and mutually rewarding relationship. The Russian elites and public are coming to terms with the fact that Romania is a member of NATO and will, soon enough, become a member of the EU too. The Romanians are also learning to see the new Russia as it really is: a dynamic power and an important regional partner.

CHAPTER FOURTEEN

Romania and Turkey: Friendship and Partnership on the Way to EU Membership[1]

Erhan İçener

The accession of Bulgaria and Romania to the European Union (EU) will complete the biggest step towards the aim of uniting Europe: eastern enlargement. However, this will not be the end of enlargement, the EU's most successful foreign policy tool to date. Although it is not rocket science to anticipate further discussions about the necessity and costs and benefits of enlargement, especially in the light of debates following the 'no' votes in the French and Dutch referenda on the Constitutional Treaty, one should not expect that the process will be halted. Though some would like to make enlargement a scapegoat for the resulting political crisis, the overwhelming success of enlargement in bringing stability and security to Europe is widely appreciated among large sections of the Eastern and Western European publics, politicians in and outside Europe, the international media and scholars. That said, a change in the dynamics of EU enlargement is to be expected, both through a toughening of conditions and a more detailed analysis of candidate countries' abilities to cope with the obligations of EU membership particularly as the

---

[1] This chapter draws on the speeches of the Romanian President, Traian Băsescu, and the Romanian Minister for Foreign Affairs, Mihai-Răzvan Ungureanu (accessed via www.presidency.ro and www.mae.ro) and interviews conducted with officials of the Romanian government, Romanian and Turkish diplomats, and officials of the European Commission. The figures and economic data come from the Turkish Ministry of Foreign Affairs (www.mfa.gov.tr), the Embassy of Romania in Turkey (www.roembtr.org), the Foreign Economic Relations Board in Turkey (www.deik.org.tr), and *Romanya İşadamları ve Yatırımcılar Rehberi 2004–2005* (Romania Businessmen and Investors Guide) published by the Turkish Businessmen Association in Romania.

EU is still trying to digest its ten – soon to be twelve – new member states and 'widening versus deepening' is back on the agenda.

The aim of uniting Europe has not been finalized and obviously there are further steps to be taken to achieve peace, stability and security in Europe and its neighbourhood. The enlargement process with the carrot of membership seems to trigger and drive reform processes across Europe. The EU has committed itself to enlarge and the Brussels European Council in June 2005 noted the need to implement commitments fully. Hence, if they fulfil the necessary conditions, Bulgaria and Romania will join the EU in 2007. Accession negotiations have been started with Turkey and Croatia and there are also other Western Balkan states – Albania, Bosnia-Herzegovina, Macedonia, and Serbia and Montenegro – which have a membership perspective as part of the Stabilisation and Association Process with the EU. At the same time, the EU is aiming to extend stability and security and prevent the emergence of new dividing lines by creating a 'ring of friends' via the European Neighbourhood Policy (ENP) on its enlarged borders. The ENP states have not, however, been granted a membership perspective. This may undermine the prospects for success of the ENP and force reconsideration, especially given the interest of some of the neighbouring states in membership. Hence, and considering global and regional challenges in and beyond Europe, discussions about the future and dynamics of EU enlargement will continue.

This chapter contributes to these discussions and analyses on EU enlargement by focusing on the impact that Romania's membership of the EU will have on its and the EU's relations with Turkey. Since the beginning of the current enlargement process, Romania has always been labelled a 'laggard'. This reflects the fact that it has been the worst performing candidate among the twelve countries negotiating accession. The persistent sense of laggardness was confirmed when enlargement proceeded in May 2004 without Romania. Although it shares in this sense the laggard label with Bulgaria, Romania is actually 'the laggard' overall in the process of eastern enlargement. While Bulgaria finished negotiating the terms of its accession with the EU in June 2004, Romania succeeded in closing the last remaining chapters on competition and justice and home affairs shortly before the end of 2004. Similarly, Turkey is lagging behind in the enlargement process. In EU statements concerning enlargement, Turkey has always stood out as the candidate yet to qualify for the opening of negotiations. Hence, Turkey was the only non-negotiating candidate until Croatia was granted candidate status in June 2004. After making unexpected progress in meeting the Copenhagen political criteria following the election of the AKP government in November 2002, accession negotiations with Turkey were eventually opened on 3 October 2005. However, the evolving dynamics of enlargement, the 'unique' discussions regarding Turkey's identity, size and geographical position, and attempts to find alternatives to membership signal that Turkey may still be 'the laggard' in the process and may ultimately find itself behind the countries of the Western Balkans and indeed others on the way towards accession. Yet, this time Turkey may not owe its status of being the 'eternal candidate', the permanent guest in the waiting room, to domestic problems but rather to an oft neglected paragraph of the Copenhagen criteria. This states that the EU should only enlarge if it has the capacity to absorb new members while maintaining the momentum of integration.

This chapter explores the possible impacts of the accession of the so-called 'laggard' of eastern enlargement – Romania – on its and the EU's relations with Turkey, 'the laggard' *par excellence* of the enlargement process to date. The chapter is divided into four sections. The first summarizes Romania-Turkey relations since 1989. The second focuses on how Romania's accession will affect relations between the two countries. The third section analyses the possible impact of Romania's accession on Turkey's membership prospects. The fourth section summarizes the arguments and offers some concluding thoughts.

ROMANIA-TURKEY RELATIONS SINCE 1989

Romania-Turkey relations have been developing in all areas since the Romanian revolution of 1989. High-level meetings between the two countries started when the late Turkish President, Turgut Özal, paid an official visit to Romania in September 1991. During this visit, Romania and Turkey signed a Treaty of Friendship, Good Neighbourhood and Cooperation. Since then, several high-level meetings have been held in both countries to strengthen collaboration and bilateral political, economic and cultural relations. As a result of these meetings, the two countries have signed a number of agreements mainly on economic issues. Among the visits conducted, two recent ones are of particular symbolic importance as signs of good relations and friendship between the two countries. First, in July 2004, the Turkish President, Ahmet Necdet Sezer, attended the 500th anniversary of the death of Prince Stephen of Moldovia – Stefan the Great – who is famous for his resistance to the Ottomans. As a tribute, Sezer brought Prince Stephen's sword, which was captured by the Turks, for temporary exhibition in Romania. Second, and in the same month, the then Romanian Prime Minister, Adrian Năstase, attended the wedding of the daughter of his Turkish counterpart, Recip Tayyip Erdoğan. The ceremony provided a special opportunity for the Turkish Prime Minister to show off his personal relationships with foreign leaders and to project Turkey as a model location for the meeting of civilizations. To this end, at the invitation of Erdoğan, the Prime Ministers of Romania and Greece, the King of Jordan and the President of Pakistan served as witnesses in the ceremony.

Romania and Turkey also cooperate in different regional and international institutions and work together to strengthen stability and security in their regions and neighbourhood. Both countries participate in regional economic, political and security organizations such as the Stability Pact for Southeastern Europe, the South East European Cooperation Process (SEECP), the Southeast European Cooperative Initiative, BLACKSEAFOR, and the Black Sea Economic Cooperation (BSEC) in order to find regional solutions to challenges facing Southeastern Europe or the Black Sea. Romania and Turkey have been members of the Organization of Security and Cooperation in Europe (OSCE) since its establishment and have long been involved in dialogue and cooperation, both during and after the Cold War. A NATO member since 1952, Turkey long offered vigorous support to Romania's application for membership. It viewed Romanian accession – as well as that of other new members – as a contribution to Euro-Atlantic security and stability. Romania's membership of NATO will provide added value to the existing international and bilateral cooperation between Romania and Turkey. Additionally, the fight against the sources of instability and threats to Euro-Atlantic security that have their roots in the wider Black Sea area are much more easily addressed with Romania and Turkey as NATO members.

Economic and commercial relations between the two countries have also been increasing constantly. Trends in political and economic relations and in Turkish investment in Romania indicate that there is considerable potential for further development in economic and commercial relations. Turks were among the first group of foreign investors to conduct business in post-revolution Romania. Currently, Turkey is Romania's most important economic partner in the Balkans. Overall, according to figures for 2004, Turkey ranks fourth after Italy, Germany and France. The volume of trade between the two countries in 2003 stood at US$1.82 billion, a figure that represented a more than 50% increase on 2002. The volume of trade subsequently reached US$3 billion in 2004 with US$4 billion being the targeted trade volume for 2005. Turkish investment in Romania amounts to around US$460 million and involves close to 9300 joint ventures. This figure rises to more than US$1 billion if investments coming from Turkish companies registered in other European countries are included.

While Turkey has a significant presence in Romanian economic life, it is difficult to say the same for the Romanian presence in Turkey. According to figures for 2004, there are only sixteen Romanian registered companies in Turkey

– twelve of which operate in the service sector – and Romania ranks 11th in terms of Turkey's export markets and 19th for imports. While Romanian exports to Turkey are raw materials, metal (iron-steel), plastic, mineral fuels, and organic chemicals, Romania's main imports from Turkey are automobiles, automotive products, machinery, electrical machinery, cotton and iron-steel products.

Turkish investment in Romania was initiated by small and medium-sized enterprises soon after 1989. Later on, Turkish investment in Romania expanded into all sectors. Turks mainly invested in banking, food sector, textiles, beer production, yeast production, electronics and construction. Additionally, Turkish holdings – such as Bayraktar, Kombassan, Yaşar, and Koç – bought shares in Romanian firms like Robank, Azomures, Rulmantul Barlad, IASMAN, and Arctic during the privatization process. The Efes Pilsen beer factory, the GİMA supermarket chain, the Pakmaya yeast factory, and the DYO paint factory are other important examples of Turkish investment in Romania. Additionally, there are several Turkish construction companies present in Romania mainly involved in road construction.

One negative among these positive developments concerns the banking sector which, in the case of Turkey at the end of 2000, experienced one of its worst financial crises ever. This was triggered by a liquidity crisis in Turkish banks and was followed by the government taking control of ten banks. The crisis worsened and Turkey struggled to reform its economy and banking sector. What was important for Turkish-Romanian relations was the damage the crisis caused for the image of Turkish banks in Romania. The activities of Banca Turco-Romana, owned by Bayındır Holding, were frozen by the National Bank of Romania. Furthermore, a decision of the Central Bank of Turkey to take control of the activities of Demirbank and Sümerbank, both of which had been operating in Romania, further undermined Romanians' trust in Turkish banks. Turkey's improved economic performance since and the success of other Turkish companies have helped to heal the damage caused. At present, there are three Turkish banks in Romania that are increasing their market share year on year: Finansbank, Garanti Bank International and Libra Bank.

Turkey's flourishing trade and investment in Romania owes its success to several factors. First, geographical proximity, excellent political relations and bilateral cooperation provide a promising framework for economic and commercial relations. Second, within this framework Romania's progress towards adopting the *acquis communautaire* in preparation for EU membership brings greater stability and predictability to a country and thus attracts Turkish entrepreneurs wishing to invest abroad. Third, Turkish citizens did not need a visa to enter Romania until 1 April 2004. The availability of visa-free travel made Romania an easier place with which to establish trade links. Fourth, agreements signed between Romania and Turkey on economic and commercial issues have helped to facilitate trade and investments. The agreements, such as those on the avoidance of double taxation (1986), on promoting and the reciprocal guarantee of investments (1991), free trade (1997), and cooperation between Eximbank SA Romania and Türk Eximbank AŞ (2004), have contributed to successful and promising economic and commercial links between the two countries. In addition to these bilateral agreements, there has been the role of and membership of regional organizations such as the SEECP and BSEC and their shared interest for the economic and political security of their region. Last, but not least, Turkish and Romanian private sector organizations play an active and effective role in enhancing economic and commercial relations and helping to solve problems affecting trade and investment. The Turkish Businessmen's Association in Romania (TİAD), the Foreign Economic Relations Board (DEİK), the Turkish-Romanian Business Council, the Turkish Industrialists' and Businessmen's Association (TUSİAD), The Union of Chambers and Commodity Exchanges in Turkey (TOBB), and The Chamber of Commerce and Industry of Romania and Bucharest Municipality (CCIRB) are leading actors promoting economic and commercial relations between Romania and Turkey.

Social and cultural relations between the two countries are also developing well. Turks and Romanians share a similar cultural and historical background mainly because of the Ottoman presence in the Balkans. Today, there are around 55,000 Turks living in Romania and they are represented as a minority in parliament. It is possible to hear Turkish words in the Romanian language, taste Turkish influence in Romanian cuisine and see examples of Ottoman architecture in the Dobrogea region. On the other side, Istanbul hosts the Saint Parascheva Church which was given to the Romanian Orthodox Community to use in 2004. Dimitrie Cantemir – Prince of Moldovia, historian, linguist, and composer – can be regarded as the figure that both Romanians and Turks hold in high regard. Although Cantemir fought against the Turks, he contributed to Turkish music and world history by writing a history book on the Ottoman Empire in the 18th Century. Good relations between the two countries in the post-1989 era also owe much to tourism and football. Turkey is a very popular destination for Romanian tourists and football players. Without doubt, this helps Turkey enhance its image and increase its coverage in the Romanian media, and in turn strengthens friendship and a sense of closeness between the peoples of the two countries.

THE IMPACT OF ROMANIA'S ACCESSION TO THE EU ON ROMANIA-TURKEY RELATIONS

The impact of Romania's accession on Romania-Turkey relations pre-dates actual membership of the EU. Given the obligation to adopt the EU *acquis*, Romania revised its visa regime and started to impose a visa requirement on Turkish citizens from 1 April 2004. This followed thirty-six years of visa-free entry. It was certainly expected that the change in the visa regime would have consequences for commercial relations and tourism. To minimize the negative consequences, the authorities reached an agreement in 2004 on reciprocal visits. This allows for the granting of short stay visas with multiple entries to businessmen and representatives of commercial companies giving them the right to stay for a maximum of ninety days in a period of six months from the date of the first entry. The basic requirement is to have a valid travel document and a letter of reference issued by the relevant chamber of commerce or other economic board in Turkey or Romania. The agreement also provided some exemptions for bus and truck drivers. On the Turkish side, and probably so as not to discourage Romanian tourists from visiting Turkey, Romania was included in the list of countries whose citizens can obtain visas at Turkish border points.

As noted, economic and commercial relations between Romania and Turkey have been developing since 1989 and the trend suggests that they will continue to do so. Romanian membership of the EU is expected to provide a stimulus for further improvement. Geographical proximity, close cultural and historical background, stable economic and political conditions, business and investment opportunities, the prospect of membership at an earlier date than Turkey are among the factors that make Romania attractive as an 'investment base' to Turkish businessmen who want to operate inside the EU. One obvious consequence of Romania's accession to the EU will be the extension of the EU-Turkey Customs Union to Romania. This will upgrade the existing free trade agreement between the parties and will see the same common external tariff applied to third countries. In addition, Turkey's continued efforts to join the EU give no reason to expect negative repercussions from Romania's accession in bilateral relations. On the contrary, the future of economic and commercial relations between the two is bright and their success is an example for other countries of the Black Sea and Balkans.

Romania's EU membership will have a constructive effect on Romania and Turkey's common efforts to bring peace, prosperity, stability and security to South Eastern Europe and the wider neighbourhood. Both countries are suffering from similar regional threats and risks. They have a common interest in fighting them and raising the importance of the threats stemming from South Eastern Europe and the Black Sea Region in international organizations. Romania and Turkey have a shared interest in and aim to support the Euro-Atlantic integration of Balkan and Black Sea countries. Here, Romania could play a significant role as an EU member in enhancing relations between BSEC, the SEECP and the EU. In a combined effort with other EU members of BSEC, Romania is expected to push relations with and a strategy for the Black Sea as a region on to the EU agenda. With common membership in several regional organizations covering political, economic, social and cultural areas, Turkey and Romania can increase their collaboration to contribute to stability and security in South Eastern Europe and beyond. Romania could lobby through its voting rights, representation and leverage inside the EU for cooperation between regional organizations. It is expected that Turkey will not hesitate to support Romania in its efforts.

In fact, Romania has already started to push for more emphasis on the wider Black Sea area. It is not an overstatement to say that since they come to power almost every speech of the Romanian President, Traian Băsescu, the Romanian Minister of Foreign Affairs, Mihai-Răzvan Ungureanu, directed to an international audience has highlighted the importance of the Black Sea region for Romania and the Euro-Atlantic community. Emphasising the geopolitical importance and unpredictable nature of the wider Black Sea area – an area that includes several frozen and ongoing conflicts – Romania wishes to play a more active role as a regional actor. All the arguments and threats presented are real. However, whether Romania is capable of playing a leading role is a matter of speculation. It can be argued that NATO is best positioned to respond. Indeed, the first NATO summit Romania attended as a member – in Turkey in June 2004 – noted the importance of the Black Sea region for Euro-Atlantic security and underlined the readiness of NATO members to complement the efforts of existing regional cooperation mechanisms.

Nevertheless, what Romania expects and the region needs are more than a promise. One can argue that if Romania looks for regional support and a partner to pursue a more active role in the Black Sea or elsewhere, Turkey is the best candidate. Considering the importance Romania gives to its strategic partnerships with the United States and the United Kingdom, especially since the last elections in December 2004, and Turkey's similar long-lasting strategic relationship with the United States, it is to be expected that Romania's NATO membership will impact more on Romania-Turkey relations than the country's membership of the EU. Romania's EU membership could though increase the support of EU institutions for policies of common interest to Romania and Turkey.

Another potential area for collaboration is the ENP. Romania as an EU member and Turkey as a candidate country negotiating accession may contribute to the success of ENP together. As countries bordering the EU's new neighbours, Romania and Turkey have additional interests in and a duty to act for the success of the ENP and can be expected to lobby for further initiatives for the region where. Therefore, Romania's EU membership may enhance existing Romanian-Turkish cooperation to promote regional security and stability.

Social and cultural relations are expected to improve following Romania's accession to the EU. New opportunities for social and cultural exchange should emerge. Clearly, there are not many opportunities and projects at present for young Romanians and Turks to get to know each other better. More exchanges between schools and universities, and common projects in cultural, social and educational areas might provide young people from both countries with opportunities to meet and explore what and how much they have in common. It would help the construction of European and regional identity and would be an important investment for overcoming misjudgements and mistaken images. Tourism definitely helps too. However, there is a need for more exchanges involving young people if a common future is to be built. This has to be done especially in the Balkans and Black Sea region where each nation's own recent past and history are full of troubles, and memories of these and 'enemies' remain fresh. It is no surprise that when an opportunity to study abroad exists Romanians and Turks would prefer the United States or a Western European country as their destination. To increase the incentives and make it more attractive, Romania's EU membership could help Romania lobby for more EU funds to increase regional social, cultural and educational exchanges among young people as well as teachers and academics. If these efforts were successful in the Balkans and the wider Black Sea area, it would definitely be a good investment for Turkey, Romania and all other participating countries.

THE IMPACT OF ROMANIA'S ACCESSION TO THE EU ON TURKEY-EU RELATIONS

Obviously, Romania's accession to the EU will not only affect Romania-Turkey relations. It will also have consequences and implications on Turkey-EU relations and Turkey's membership prospects. At the moment, like many of the new members of the EU, Romania is reiterating its support for Turkey's membership aspirations and for the continuation of its accession process. It is expected that the new members will not oppose any accession process so soon after gaining entry to the EU. It would be morally wrong and against their interests given that enlargement brings stability to Europe. However, it is widely recognized that Turkish accession will take time and there will be ongoing discussions on the costs and benefits of its accession for the EU and beyond. Therefore, although there is support today for the process, in due time Romania's preferences and position may change.

Some in the EU expect the new member states to be both neutral in important strategic discussions and more pro-EU than Atlanticist in foreign policy choices. Indeed, Romania was strongly criticised during the crisis over Iraq in 2003 when it sought to combine strong support for the US with a commitment to 'Europeanness'. On Turkish accession it is expected that Romania will be neutral before joining since it has nothing to gain by expressing opposition. Once it has become a member, however, Romania will have a voice and votes. Turkish diplomats do not think that Romania will be among the countries that may cause difficulties over Turkey's accession. Yet, Romania's accession will unavoidably have some effects both on Turkey-EU relations and the EU enlargement process.

Since finalizing its accession to NATO and the EU, Romania has started to look for a role to play in these organizations by emphasising its geopolitical situation. Being on the edge of the new EU, Romania has revived its old mythical 'function of defender of European civilization'.[2] However, this time Romania wants to defend Europe not by resisting outsiders but by engaging with the Western Balkans and playing a bridging role in promoting democratization and europeanization in the EU's neighbourhood. This can be done through the ENP and, in Romanian eyes, the development of a new security concept for the wider Black Sea area.[3]

It should be noted that the arguments Romania puts forward in support of an active Black Sea area policy are exactly the same as those used by the Turks to underline the geopolitical importance of their accession to the EU. When Romania highlights the threats stemming from wider Black Sea area and the need to promote stability in the region for the security of Europe and energy routes, it strengthens the Turkish case. According to supporters of Turkish accession and many Turks, Turkey would be an asset to the EU in its efforts to remove the sources of instability in its neighbourhood. Nonetheless, it is questionable whether indeed it is necessary to admit Turkey to the EU in order to play such roles since it is already a NATO member and has no interest at all in undermining the EU's efforts to democratize and stabilize its neighbourhood.

---

[2] See Boia, L. *History and Myth in Romanian Consciousness* (Budapest: Central European University Press, 2001), p.156.

[3] See Asmus, R.D. et al (eds.), *A New Euro-Atlantic Strategy for the Black Sea Region* (Washington D.C.: German Marshall Fund, 2004).

Moreover, the difficulties of being an EU border country and Romania's insistence on the need to promote European involvement in securing the long-term stability of the wider Black Sea area suggest that Romania will continue to support an open-door policy for the EU.[4] Such support for ongoing enlargement into the Western Balkans and Europe's wider neighbourhood may affect Turkey-EU relations in two ways. First, it is clear from the statements of successive Romanian Ministers of Foreign Affairs that Romania does not relish the prospect of being 'on the edge of Europe'.[5] Therefore, Romania is expected to support Turkey's accession in order that the EU's border can be pushed further east thereby reducing the burden on Romania and allowing the country to feel a little bit more like an 'insider'. Turkish accession would also help reduce challenges associated with organized crime, the trafficking of humans, drug trafficking and weapon smuggling stemming from the wider Black Sea area.

Second, however, Romania may prioritise the accession of the Western Balkan states and Moldova. Speeches by President Băsescu and the Minister for Foreign Affairs, Mihai-Răzvan Ungureanu, on EU enlargement and foreign policy issues demonstrate how much importance they give to the Western Balkans and Moldova. Indeed, Băsescu has argued that Europe needs a break from enlargement and that its next priority should be the Western Balkans. On the question of Turkey, and after emphasising the friendship that exists between Romania and Turkey, Băsescu stated that although the opening of accession negotiations in October 2005 would be welcome, the speed with which Turkey and indeed Ukraine could join the EU would depend on the EU's capacity to absorb more members. He continued by arguing that for the moment a privileged partnership would be an acceptable compromise both for the EU and for Turkey and Ukraine.[6]

Although Băsescu's comments on the EU's capacity to absorb new members like Turkey are fair, they do suggest that Romanian support for Turkish accession cannot be taken for granted. Also, Turks may have difficulty in under-standing the coupling with Ukraine at the time when accession negotiations are taking place and Ukraine is not even a candidate. A privileged partnership, a concept without content and undefined status, might be an 'acceptable

---

[4] Ungureanu, M.R. *EU Enlargement: Where Next for the EU's Borders?*, Speech at the Chatham House, London, 20 June 2005 (via www.mae.ro/index.php?unde=doc&id=10513&idlnk=2&cat=4).

[5] Geoana, M.D. *Romania: The Last Lap Towards EU Accession*, European Policy Centre: Communication to Members, S31/04, 16 April 2004. Note also the comments of Mihai-Răzvan Ungureanu (*op cit*) that 'no border country likes to be a border country'.

[6] 'Eine politische Union braucht eine Verfassung', *Frankfurter Allgemeine Zeitung*, 6 July 2005 (via www.faz.net). See also 'President Băsescu rejects idea that Romania's accession to EU could be delayed for one year', *ROMPRES,* 6 July 2005 (via http://ue.mae.ro).

compromise' for Ukraine and the EU 'at the moment'. However, not only friends of Turkey but even 'the deaf Sultan', as Turks would say, have heard that Turks see themselves 'privileged' enough with their current associate status and customs union. Furthermore, Turkish authorities repeat at every occasion that nothing less than membership is or will be acceptable for them 'at the moment' or in the future.

Because there will probably be a decade between Romania's accession and when Turkey hopes to finalize its accession negotiations, Turkey will not be directly affected by Romania's accession in the way that Romania was affected by the accession of the ten countries that joined the EU in May 2004. On the other hand, Turkey's accession process will definitely be affected by enlargement fatigue and the problems the EU-15 have had to cope with in admitting twelve new members. There is little about which Turkey can complain. Instead, it should focus on preparing itself as best it can for accession. Here, Romania's experiences, at times problematic, could be advantageous for Turkey if there were an exchange of information. Being a country with a large agricultural sector, with problems concerning corruption, its justice system and the environment, Romania may be an example for Turkey and assist Turkey in its efforts to address the challenges it will face during the negotiations.

SUMMARY AND CONCLUSION

Romania and Turkey are partners in the Balkan and Black Sea regions. They have very good bilateral political and economic relationships. The future for these relations is encouraging. Moreover, the Euro-Atlantic integration of Romania will enhance existing cooperation between the two countries in several regional organizations. Both countries have an interest in promoting stability and security in the Balkans, the Black Sea and beyond. At this point, Romania's accession to NATO can be regarded as a very important development for upgrading existing cooperation. As both countries are members of NATO, it will be easier for them to work together and obtain the support of other important international actors. Although economic ties form the core of Romanian-Turkish bilateral relations, security-related issues dominate the agenda of both countries' foreign policies. They also arguably provide the rationale for their accession to the EU and its timing. Both countries have a strategic relationship with the United States and it is fair to say that the United Kingdom is the most consistent supporter of their EU accession processes. Both countries face the same challenges at the border of the EU and in their neighbourhood. Thus, it is expected that Romania and Turkey will continue to collaborate at every possible occasion.

Moreover, Romania's attempts to construct a new security concept in the wider Black Sea region may highlight the importance of Turkey's accession to the EU. The arguments Romania has been putting forward for the realization of this policy should remind those who are sceptical of Turkish membership how important Turkey is for the Middle East, Balkans, Black Sea and Caucasus regions. This may lead to a re-evaluation of the costs and benefits of accepting Turkey as a member of the EU or of linking it firmly through a close bond with the EU.

To conclude, Romania's accession to the EU will mainly have positive effects. On the other hand, it might be an exaggeration to suggest that Romania will be an influential player inside the EU and that its accession will directly affect EU-Turkey relations. But, Romania's accession will have indirect effects on Turkey-EU relations. For instance, Romania could share its experiences with Turkey and provide advice on the challenges Turkey will face during accession negotiations and in implementing its obligations. This may help Turkey's europeanization. Collaboration in other international and regional organizations will provide the basis for further cooperation. For sure, discussions on the future of the EU will affect the possibility of Turkey acceding to the EU. Romania may have its own priorities for EU enlargement; it is not, however, likely that Romania will openly oppose Turkish membership. On the contrary, reflecting upon its own experiences and the likely benefits coming from Turkey's accession, Romania can be expected to support Turkey's membership aspirations. What more can Turkey ask from a friend and partner which it robustly supported during debates on NATO enlargement?

CHAPTER FIFTEEN

EU and the Western Balkans: the Challenges of the Pre-accession Process

Othon Anastasakis

The prospect of the accession of Romania and Bulgaria to the European Union (EU) in 2007 or 2008 opens the gate for the Balkan countries. Suddenly, the integration of the region into the EU becomes more tangible and the accession of the Western Balkan countries a more credible possibility. Notwithstanding the EU's post-enlargement fatigue, the constitutional doom and gloom and the budgetary disagreements between EU member states, the autumn of 2005 marked a notable advance in the relations of the EU with South East Europe. Croatia and Turkey started accession negotiations on 3 October; Serbia and Montenegro (SiM) started negotiations on a Stabilisation and Association Agreement (SAA) on 10 October; Bosnia and Herzegovina (BiH) was given the green light to start SAA negotiations too; the Former Yugoslav Republic (FYR) of Macedonia received a positive avis from the Commission on its membership application and later candidate status from the European Council; and Albania was considered ready to sign a SAA. The enlargement agenda was gaining some momentum and the EU seemed willing to supply more commitment, engagement and closer association to the Western Balkan countries.[1]

While all this conveys a sense of inevitability as far as the European integration of the Western Balkans is concerned, it all depends on whether the backward and conflict-prone Western Balkan countries will ever be ready for membership. In the minds of most people the answer lies with the EU which

---

[1] See the speech of the Commissioner for Enlargement, Olli Rehn, to the Foreign Affairs Committee of the European Parliament on 21 June 2005, in which he introduced his Plan 'C' for enlargement aiming at: consolidation, conditionality and communication. The speech is available via http://europa.eu.int/comm/commission_barroso/rehn/speeches/speeches_en.htm.

has proved to have an overwhelming impact on candidate and potential candidate countries. As a matter of fact, the Western Balkan region is now moving gradually and slowly towards a pre-accession framework (with the exception of Croatia which is conducting accession negotiations and hoping to become a member as soon as possible). Having transferred the Western Balkans' European integration agenda to the European Commission's Directorate-General (DG) for Enlargement the EU appears more committed to pursue their transformation on the basis of the accession process.

This chapter addresses briefly – and bearing in mind Romania's integration with the EU – some of the challenges facing the EU in its effort to bring the Western Balkan region closer to the norms and practices of the club. These include: first, how to use lessons from the eastern enlargement experience; second, how to manage the multiple speeds in the region; third, how to deal with regional uncertainty; and fourth, how to handle a wide-ranging agenda. Without underestimating the importance of local actors in the process, the Europeanization of the region largely depends on how the EU responds to these challenges in the current pre-accession and the subsequent accession phases.

LESSONS FROM THE EASTERN ENLARGEMENT EXPERIENCE: OLD VERSUS NEW RECIPES

With varying degrees of success, the EU can claim to have contributed to the transformation of all the new Central and East European (CEE) members. Being a path dependent entity, the EU learns from its own experience with member states and candidate countries, and applies lessons learned to subsequent cases. It uses its strongest card – the enlargement instrument – and combines this with financial assistance to help the countries through this adaptation process, and applies the same conditionality, already introduced with previous post-communist transition candidates. From then on, the EU is also free to introduce more obligations, to set up new financial instruments, to add further conditions,[2] and/or to interpret the existing conditionality in the way it sees fit for each individual case.

A comparison of the Western Balkans with the CEE countries entails some obvious similarities as well as striking differences. Undoubtedly, all the countries set off from the same starting point: the collapse of communism and facing similar transition challenges. Yet, they also developed fundamental

---

[2]   The Western Balkan environment has led to the addition of new conditions including full cooperation with the ICTY, respect for minority rights, the return of refugees and displaced persons, and a commitment to regional cooperation.

differences during the transition process itself. Each country pursued its own national path towards European integration with varying degrees of success. The example of Romania, in particular, can offer some relevant insights as to how to deal with complicated cases of reform and reluctant domestic politics. The former Yugoslav countries are the product of ethnic conflict, war and fragmentation that has altered the local rules of the game substantially. For the most part, they are young countries with undefined boundaries, inexperienced elites, weak states, unskilled administrations, backward economies and disaffected populations. This is a drastically different regional context from that of Central Europe, and raises questions regarding the relevance of post-communist enlargement recipes. Are, for instance, the economic formulas that have worked in Central Europe appropriate for the post-conflict needs of the Western Balkans? What kind of market reforms should the EU promote in the region? Can their weak administrations manage the implementation of demanding EU laws? How much and what kind of state intervention is required? How can the weak and illegitimate central structures be strengthened? What kind of decentralisation and regional policy is required in these ethnically divided territories? Do the Western Balkan states have the absorption capacity to benefit from structural funds? And, overall, if there are significant differences between Central Europe and the Balkans, how far should the EU deviate from its own norms and practices to accommodate regional particularities?

Every accession process is designed and based on the model of previous cases. But with each category of applicants the EU is faced with a new experience and has to adapt the conditions, criteria and goals to suit the particularities of the new environment. Eastern enlargement, itself was very different from the 1980s southern enlargement and the lessons from the Spanish, Portuguese or Greek experience had limited value for post-communist Europe. Similarly, the Western Balkan region added post-conflict reconstruction and development as dimensions of the enlargement process, differing considerably from the Central European and Baltic experience. To accommodate such challenges, the EU might have to introduce some recipes that help the future candidate countries address their specific needs and help them catch up with the increasingly demanding requirements of the EU. Yet, what eastern enlargement teaches us is that there has to be commitment on the part of the European Commission to tackle all the difficult issues during the pre-accession and accession process. This is the major lesson from the Romanian example, where the EU, despite its criticism and concern over the pace of reform, kept its commitment intact throughout the whole process.

MANAGING REGIONAL DIVERSITY: BILATERAL VERSUS REGIONAL ENGAGEMENT

Despite the limited geographical space and the common Yugoslav background, there are differences among the successor countries in their level of development, their degree of integration with the EU and their capacity for membership. Each Western Balkan state is on a different rung of the EU ladder, as a result of its different domestic political and economic situation. Croatia is the most advanced case, projecting a more efficient state capacity and a class of knowledgeable technocrats. Its elites, even among the Croatian Democratic Union (HDZ) party, are more reform-minded although many still react to issues like full cooperation with the International Criminal Tribunal for the former Yugoslavia (ICTY) or other sensitive national matters. Its economy is in a better shape and reflects its much higher GDP, more inflow of foreign direct investment (FDI) and a better environment for investment.[3] FYR Macedonia, second in line, is a mixed case where fragile internal politics co-exist with local elites compliant with external conditionality. It has an inefficient state administration and inexperienced civil servants who nevertheless demonstrate a willingness to engage with the EU. While local elites and populations are divided along ethnic lines – with ethnic Macedonians trying to preserve their preponderance on national matters and ethnic Albanians seeking to achieve as many minority gains as possible – they also tend to show restrain. The November 2004 referendum on the re-territorialisation of the country showed that the majority of the people were trying to abide by the rules of the Ohrid Agreement.[4] In fact, it was compliance with the Ohrid Agreement which led the European Commission to express a positive avis on the country's application for membership despite the negative domestic economic environment and acute problems of corruption. Serbia, Montenegro and Kosovo are crucial for the normalisation of the region, constituting the unsolved border puzzle of former Yugoslavia. Serbia has the potential to change, the human capital to deliver and the international experience to negotiate but not enough political will: its rulers are polarised, its administration is corrupt and its constitutional question remains open.[5] The Serbian economy, a strong national card, has the potential to grow and the country's size can attract FDI,

[3]   Centre for Eastern Studies, *Review of the Economic Development in the Western Balkan States* (Warsaw: Centre for Eastern Studies, 2005).

[4]   International Commission on the Balkans, *The Balkans in Europe's Future* (Sofia: Centre for Liberal Studies , 2005).

[5]   Anastasakis, O. 'Democratic Transition in Serbia and the Road to Europe; Two Steps Forward, One Step Back', in Hayoz, N. et al (eds) *Enlarged EU – Enlarged Neighbourhood. Perspectives of the European Neighbourhood Policy* (Bern: Peter Lang, 2005), pp. 311–326.

once investors perceive that the local situation is functional and predictable. Similarly, the legal and administrative context will be more inviting once the ambiguities surrounding the constitutional framework are resolved. Serbia's relationship to Montenegro has been the major stumbling block in the country's Europeanisation. The EU's decision to adopt a dual-track approach with regard to the Stabilisation and Association Process (SAP) for Serbia and Montenegro illustrates how impossible it was for the two republics to converge with each other on trade or customs matters. Undoubtedly, Kosovo is the weakest regional link with limited or no experience of self-rule, a heavy-handed international administration and unreformed nationalists as local rulers. It has a very backward and barely self-sustaining economy with unemployment rates of around 60–70 per cent, the main source for its social instability. Bosnia-Herzegovina, a microcosm of former Yugoslavia, has survived the Dayton era due to intense international interference and the iron will of its High Representatives. The country is in need of strong and legitimate central structures, as the Dayton constitution was unable to provide for efficient government which would promote the reforms required by the EU. In its 2003 feasibility study the EU required 16 particular priorities to be fulfilled before the country could start talks for a SAA.[6] These were achieved in 2005 but only through the heavy handed interference of the fourth High Representative, Paddy Ashdown, a practice which generated a lot of criticism and caused internal alienation.[7] The implementation of all these new central laws will be one of the main factors that will determine the progress of relations with the EU. Finally, Albania is not a post-conflict society by Western Balkan standards but a state with all the predicaments of democratic illiberalism, economic backwardness, an inefficient and corrupt state sector, and very weak civil society.

In principle, the EU conducts its relations bilaterally by assessing each case according to its own merits. As a result, the Western Balkans' diversity is reflected in the multiple speeds of bilateral association with the EU. Relations vary from the accession negotiations currently conducted with Croatia to Kosovo's weak and poorly defined relations, the other countries being some-where in between. Yet developments in the region are also interconnected and whatever happens to one country affects some other part of the region in a positive or negative way. All the countries demonstrate similar political or socio-economic features, having been – with the exception of Albania – part

---

[6] See European Commission, *Working Paper: Bosnia-Herzegovina – Stabilisation and Association Report* 2003, SEC(2003) 340, Brussels, 26 March 2003.

[7] On the former see European Stability Initiative, *After the Bonn Powers – Open Letter to Lord Ashdown*, 16 July 2003 (via www.esiweb.org/pdf/esi_document_id_60.pdf).

of the same country before: issues like corrupt administrations, judicial deficits or economic backwardness are common to all of these states; organised crime, informal cooperation, inadequate infrastructure are shared and intertwined regional concerns.[8] This commonality and interconnectedness of issues has led the EU to adopt a regional strategy, alongside a bilateral framework, and to impose for the first time the condition of regional cooperation, not necessarily in order to achieve more trade and regional economic integration but in order to enforce some common rules of cooperation, which are also compatible with those of the EU.[9] It also supports, with greater success, cross-border co-operation projects, the development of border regions, and the funding of regional infrastructure. But there are limits to how far the EU can act regionally, given that it is primarily used to conducting enlargement processes on a bilateral basis. The co-existence between the EU and the Stability Pact revealed several weaknesses at the level of coordination and division of labour between the two.[10] In view of this bilateral/regional tension in the Western Balkans, the EU's major challenge is to manage the different national capacities and multiple speeds of integration in a context of regional inclusion in order to generate positive spillover and healthy competition towards the goal of EU membership.

TACKLING REGIONAL INSECURITY: TACTICAL VERSUS CONDITIONAL APPROACH

The Western Balkan region is characterised by uncertainty in the future, fear of regression to nationalistic and extremist practices, and the danger of a negative domino effect if or when things become rough in unstable parts of the region. The 1990s experience and the sequencing of crises and ethnic wars from one republic to the next weighed heavily in the way Westerners perceive the region. Although the situation has stabilised and there has been some degree of normalisation in recent years, there are still pockets of insecurity, unsolved national questions that have the potential to trigger renewed conflicts. Moreover, populations are generally disaffected with the political process and the lack of economic opportunities, and could thus divert their anger to more

---

[8] Anastasakis, O. and Bojicic-Dzelilovic, V. *Balkan Regional Co-operation and European Integration* (London: Hellenic Observatory – London School of Economics, 2002).

[9] Anastasakis, O. 'EU policy of regional cooperation in South East Europe: The creation of a virtual reality', *Fornet: CFSP Forum*, 3 (2) 2005, 10–12 (via www.fornet.info).

[10] see Anastasakis and Bojicic-Dzelilovic, op cit.

aggressive forms of action.[11] Important constitutional and political questions remain unsolved and the policy of constructive ambiguity, which guided EU thinking after 1999, has borne limited fruits. No one is satisfied with the progress of 'standards before status' in Kosovo, the functionality of Serbia and Montenegro as one state, or the capacity of the Dayton constitution to keep Bosnia-Herzegovina together. In the long run, there are additional worries concerning a Greater Albania, a Greater Serbia or the endurance of Macedonia.

Within this uncertain environment, the EU has to think tactically and strategically when it uses enlargement; it must offer some carrots in order to avoid the deterioration of a situation. As with the CEE cases, there are often pre-emptive intentions behind the progress with candidate countries. This happened in Romania in 1999, when the EU decided to start accession talks as a result of the Kosovo crisis and not as a result of Romania's actual progress in meeting the criteria. Similarly, the advance of relations witnessed in the autumn of 2005, did not reflect solely the progress of the Western Balkan countries, but pre-emptive thinking in order to avoid further crises and regression to nationalism and extremism. By advancing the SAP and anchoring the countries more firmly to the EU, the latter expects to seduce and co-opt local elites, offer some hope to local populations and create a more predictable environment for international investors. Naturally, there is also the reactive way in which the EU responds, closely linked with the actual monitoring and assessment of internal improvements. This reactive – rewarding or punishing – dimension is based on principles and rules, and is the result of progress in meeting conditions and criteria set out by the EU and other international institutions.[12]

The progress in the relationship of the Western Balkan countries with the EU is (and has to be) the product of tactical as well as conditional thinking, of pre-emptive as well as reactive assessment. The experience with Romania is particularly significant: strategic and other tactical considerations weighed heavily in the decision to start accession negotiations in 2000 with a country whose preparedness was largely in doubt at the time.[13] In the conflict-prone and uncertain Western Balkan region, keeping the balance between pre-emption and reaction is a very delicate exercise. The crucial challenge for the

---

[11] Krastev, I. 'The Balkans: Democracy without choices', *Journal of Democracy,* 13 (3) 2002, 39–53

[12] Smith, K.E. *The Use of Political Conditionality in the EU's Relations with Third Countries: How Effective?* EUI Working Paper SPS no. 97/7, European University Institute, Florence, 1997

[13] Phinnemore, D. 'And we would like to thank....Romania's integration into the European Union, 1987–2007', paper presented at the UACES 34th Annual Conference and 10th Research Conference, *The European Union: Past and Future Enlargements,* Zagreb, 5–7 September 2005.

EU is to be tactical when needed but without jeopardising the conditions for accession and its own high standards.

HANDLING A WIDE AGENDA: CO-ORDINATION OF DIFFERENT INSTRUMENTS

One major innovation in the EU's association with the Western Balkans has to do with the size of the agenda and the diversity of issues. The EU is thus engaged in conflict management, the reconstruction of war-torn territories, nation-building, state-building, post-communist transition to democracy and market economy, and the transposition of the *acquis communautaire*. Juggling with all those issues, the EU uses various instruments which at times are difficult to combine. As a result, the convergence of the Western Balkan countries is conducted by a number of actors, instruments and local representation offices. DG-Enlargement deals with the political, economic and technical requirements of the SAP. CARDS and its replacement, the Instrument of Pre-accession Assistance (IPA), manage the financial arena. The Common Foreign and Security Policy (CFSP) engages with high politics questions such as political relations between states or state creation i.e. constitution-making in Serbia and Montenegro and the Ohrid Agreement in FYR Macedonia. Meanwhile, the European Security and Defence Policy has been involved in military and police missions, constituting the first tests ever of the EU's ability to react more actively on the ground in security and defence matters. While there is necessity for a division of labour within the EU in order to address all the different issues, there are often problems of co-ordination among the different actors and instruments, each pursuing their own goals. For example, the introduction of a 'twin-track' approach for Serbia and Montenegro offered by the European Commission in order to facilitate the integration of the two entities, in many ways exposed CFSP insistence on keeping the state together at any cost. The challenge of the EU is to co-ordinate its own instruments in the pursuit of common and compatible goals for the region and its integration.

On various occasions, the EU has been criticised by regional experts on the effectiveness of its regional instruments and its plans in the Western Balkans. It has been accused of moving too slowly and being reluctant to commit funds, for introducing too heavy a conditionality on very weak partners, for being too feeble and indecisive, as well as for not using all the instruments of the pre-accession process like the structural funds.[14] It has also been held to account

---

[14] European Stability Initiative, *Breaking out of the Balkan Ghetto: Why IPA should be changed?*, 1 June 2005 (via www.esiweb.org/pdf/esi_document_id_66.pdf).

for not explicitly promising EU membership. This criticism reflects the slow progress in the region and the inability of the EU to act effectively and be the strong and decisive partner in this very unequal and asymmetric partnership.[15] At times, however, far too much is expected from the EU in the pursuit of a very wide agenda. This is because we tend to forget that the EU is not a nation-builder, hardly a state-builder, nor can all governmental policies be designed exclusively from outside. The EU type of state-building regards the state primarily as an agency that should deal with the implementation of the *acquis communautaire*, rather than as the interaction of the state with its citizens. This is a static and more technical understanding of the state which assumes that once efficiency is attained a country is automatically democratic and legitimate. In addition, the EU is not a development agency; at times the criticism is even levelled that its policies and demands go against the developmental needs of the poor economies of the Balkans. The EU is not a panacea for all local problems although it can suggest solutions, impose templates and conditions and offer resources to back them up.

CONCLUSION

The variety of challenges the EU faces in the Western Balkans is overwhelming as far as the europeanisation and European integration of those countries is concerned. It will take a number of years before the backward and inexperienced Western Balkan countries are ready for membership. To meet those challenges, the EU has to have a sense of purpose and vision for the future. The fourth Copenhagen criteria on the readiness of the EU to accept more members is often neglected. So far it has been taken for granted that the EU can accommodate more members and that its enlargement instrument can have benevolent repercussions for both the EU and the candidate countries. Yet, the digestion of eastern enlargement and the prospect of Turkish membership have already generated turmoil inside the EU. Even Romania's membership, notwithstanding some notable successes at the political, ethnic and economic levels, raises doubts as to whether the EU is lowering its standards in its effort to accommodate more enlargements. European publics and their leaders are rather confused as to what is the meaning and the benefits of the enlargement process. In many ways, the biggest challenge is within the EU itself; solving its own existential question will help address all of the difficult Balkan questions.

[15] Anastasakis, O. 'The Europeanization of the Balkans' *The Brown Journal of World Affairs*, 12 (1) 2005, pp. 77–88.